The Spirit Master

THE SPIRIT MASTER

JOHN SHEA

Allen, Texas

Grateful Acknowledgment is made for permission to quote copyrighted material from:

Scripture texts used in this work are taken from the *New American Bible,* copyright © 1970 by the Confraternity of Christian Doctrine, Washington, D. C., and are used by license of said copyright holder. No part of the *New American Bible* may be reproduced in any form without permission in writing. All rights reserved.

The Love of Jesus and the Love of Neighbor by Karl Rahner. English translation copyright © 1983 by The Crossroad Publishing Company. Reprinted by permission of the publisher.

"The Baby Stops Crying" and "The Diamond" from *The Song of the Bird* by Anthony de Mello, copyright © 1982. Published by Image Books, A Division of Doubleday & Company, Inc. Reprinted by permission.

True Resurrection by H. A. Williams, copyright © 1972. Published by Templegate Publishers, Springfield, IL. Used by permission.

The Color Purple by Alice Walker, copyright © 1981. Published by Harcourt Brace Jovanovich. Used by permission.

"The Journey of the Magi" in *Collected Poems 1909-1962 by* T. S. Eliot, copyright © 1936 by Harcourt Brace Jovanovich, Inc.; copyright © 1963, 1964 by T. S. Eliot. Reprinted by permission of the publisher.

Zen and the Bible by J. K. Kadowaki, copyright © 1980 by J. K. Kadowaki. Used by permission of the publishers, Routledge and Kegan Paul, London.

Cover Design by Karen Malzeke-McDonald

Send all inquiries to:
Thomas More® Publishing
200 East Bethany Drive
Allen, Texas 75002–3804

Printed in the United States of America

ISBN 0–88347–206–6

4 5 6 7 8 00 99 98 97 96

Contents

Preface

On Throwing Your Arms Around Jesus

Once I was having a conversation with a modern Protestant theologian whose theories . . . seemed to me rather rationalistic . . . At one point I put in with, "Yes, you see, you're actually only really dealing with Jesus when you throw your arms around him and realize right down to the bottom of your being that this is something you can still do today."

And my theologian replied, "Yes, you're right, of course—if you don't mean it too pietistically."[1]

Karl Rahner

One of the things I do to stay out of trouble or, from another perspective, to get into trouble, is theological reflection. To put it more technically, I facilitate and resource groups of Christians, mainly Catholics, as they reflect on their experience in the light of their faith in order to act more effectively and creatively. This activity goes on in church basements and living rooms as well as in learning centers and classrooms. Over the years I have found myself in all these places, and more.

I would like to use a few reflections from this activity as a springboard into the concerns of this book.

When it comes to theological reflection, people are enamored of method. They want to know the three steps ("Are we in step two now?") that will bring them theological clarity and inner peace. But the truth is that the process of theological reflection entails a series of tentative guesses and spontaneous moves which may or may not unleash the spirit of the individual and group. The simplest move of all, especially if the group is ministers, is to ask: "What are some of the beliefs that guide your life?"

People come up with beliefs in all areas—God, culture, human nature, wealth, right and wrong behavior, death, and so on. After these beliefs are "on the table," another move is required. One of the questions which provokes an interesting discussion is "Why do you believe these things?" The responses usually fall into two categories. People believe things because they are part of their experience and because if they hold on to these beliefs, life will be better. These people are basically empiricists and pragmatists. Experience and consequences are what make a difference.

I often ask, "Are there any other reasons why you might believe these things?" All these people are Christians, and this group has been convened explicitly to do theological reflection. So naturally I am fishing for some connection to the resources of the tradition. Although theological reflection can be done without reference to a religious tradition, it is extremely difficult, and the yield at the end is definitely not a hundredfold. What I hope to hear is "It's in the Bible" or "It's part of our Creed" or "Jesus says something about that, doesn't he?" More often than not I have to supply the connection and the content.

I know that if I would hang around with Protestant fundamentalists or charismatic Catholics, that would not be the case. Scripture quotes would fill the air. Or if I would meet more often with "traditionalists," there would be no shortage of references to the tradition, especially conciliar statements and papal encyclicals. But the groups I am part of are avowedly secular Christians, with the accent on secular. And there is a very good reason why this is the crowd that I find myself with. I am one of them.

I began to pay special attention to "when and how" Jesus entered the conversation. Sometimes he did not make an appearance at all. At other times, he made an appearance, but he did not carry much weight. If a Jesus story was introduced at a critical juncture in the discussion, it did not get a lot of air time, and there was no sustained effort to penetrate its meaning and apply it. More often than not, Jesus was an afterthought. After the group had agreed on some value, a Jesus story was brought in for support. All in all, Jesus was another ingredient in the mix. He fought for attention alongside personal experience, culture, reason, Scripture, and theology.

This bothered me, but I was not sure why. Certainly I did not want the Jesus material to be a "close down." A "close down" happens when something is introduced that has so much authority in the lives of the people that the conversation comes to a halt under the weight of that opinion. Every group can be closed down. Depending on the participants, "the Pope says . . . ," "Scripture says . . . ," "Karl Rahner says . . . ," "the pastor says . . . " can suddenly silence a group. Excessive deference kills creative conversation and strategy. I did not want Jesus to be so well thought of that nobody else thought in his presence. In fact, it was just the opposite. I wanted his presence, mediated through his story, to be the catalyst of original perspectives and startling actions.

I also thought the reason Jesus was not getting a sufficient hearing was poor hermeneutics. I used to joke about the ways people merged the Gospels with contemporary life. Jesus whipped the money changers out of the Temple; therefore, we should roust the ushers. Jesus was not a zealot; therefore, Christians should not be politically active. Jesus ate with tax collectors and sinners; therefore, we should throw a party and invite the IRS and prostitutes. These mechanical transpositions from Jesus' time to our own are ludicrous. They do not recognize historical distance and blithely attempt connections that never really connect. These muddled efforts to make Jesus a real influence hurt his credibility.

There is no doubt that what is needed is a more sophisticated way of relating the Scriptures to contemporary experience. But the difficulty is deeper than that. When we brought the Jesus story into the conversation, there was no personal allegiance to him and his story. When Christian faith is considered from an objective standpoint, everything hinges on Jesus Christ. An organic understanding of the tradition must make the life, death, and resurrection of Jesus central to Christian faith. Therefore, I felt obliged on theological grounds to touch base with Jesus. Any reflection on experience from the perspective of Christian faith should have a christological component. So my question was "How would you approach this from a Jesus perspective?"

This question, put to a hundred groups, brought home in a new way one of the foundational distinctions of religious traditions. Theological reflection is second-order activity. It presupposes more primary religious experiences which have generated faith perspectives and values. Theology explores and extends these perspectives and values into all the areas of human life. Therefore, the persuasiveness of the theology is at least partially dependent on the persuasiveness of the underlying religious experience.

Theology without some foundational religious experience as its energy and direction is empty activity. It is also wrongheaded activity. Without the "sense of salvation" which the religious experience provides, theology becomes abstract, ideological, and insensitive. Leonardo Boff says, "A theology—any theology—not based on spiritual experience is mere panting—religious breathlessness."[2] Herwig Arts expresses the same insight a little more imaginatively: "Without experience the mind is a mill grinding without grain."[3]

So if we are doing Christian theological reflection, it is presupposed that we have had a spiritual experience mediated through Jesus. This can happen in many ways. But the important thing is that it does happen and that it happens a number of times in the course of a Christian's life. Fresh salvific encounters with God and neighbor through Jesus is salt for a bland diet and leaven for a flat life. It also makes Christology reasonable activity. Naturally, I want to know more about the person who has affected me in this way. Also, and this is a certainty, he may have more to say.

Therefore, commitment to the outcome of Christian theological reflection is directly related to these more primary encounters with Jesus. If through Jesus people had found a power that had made them and others flourish, they struggled with how to integrate what Jesus had to say into their lives. If there had not been a significant encounter with Jesus, he was the burden they carried rather than the blessing they delighted in. They knew about him, but they did not know he knew about them. They obligingly listened to what he had to say, but they did not hold that high expectation that he would change their minds and hearts. Indebtedness to Jesus must precede and inform any Christian theology which hopes to be vital and engaging.

The classic path to these more primary encounters with Jesus is through direct contact with the creations of the Christian tradition. Christian liturgy—the myth and ritual which emerged from the Jesus event—makes Jesus Christ eternally present.[4] Also the reality of Jesus Christ can be encountered through the community, its leaders, and the many liturgical, devotional, and ascetical practices which surround and reflect the central mysteries. The multiple creations of the Christian tradition are, on one hand, expressions of the encounter with Jesus Christ and, on the other hand, are meant to lead people back to the experience of Jesus Christ.

Many think this mediatory role of Christian creations is not "working" well. Community, authority, word, sacrament, and all their companions are not functioning sacramentally. They are not facilitating a primary encounter with Jesus Christ. But my guess is that for most people they still provide genuine sacramental encounters with Jesus.

A much-favored contemporary path to an encounter with Jesus Christ reserves the creations of the Christian tradition for an important but secondary role. They are brought forward to articulate and critique the findings of contemporary experience. They do not mediate an encounter with Jesus Christ; they subsequently interpret his implicit presence in the seemingly secular flow of events. The flow of faith moves from contemporary experience to Christian interpretation.

Secular people have religiously significant experiences which put them in contact with the ultimate Mystery of human existence. These experiences may be triggered by nature, birth, death, or sexual attraction. They may also occur in the context of interpersonal love, commitment to truth, a passion for justice, and friendship. But without the help of the Christian symbols, and the Jesus story in particular, the fullness of these experiences, both in their creative and demonic dimensions, is missed. People's primary encounter with Jesus is as the interpretive voice that tells them the truth of what they have undergone.

Both these paths provide a primary encounter with the reality of Jesus Christ. The expected outcome is that the person becomes a believer. The experiences are distilled into truths, a process that the Catholic tradition highly prizes, and the truths become touchstones for a way of life. The truths which the encounter with Jesus has generated are magnificent, and when they come together, they create a vision of God, self, neighbor, society, and universe which is thrilling. It grounds our capacity to celebrate, repent, enter agreements, both embrace and transcend the earth, suffer, die, and hope. From my prejudiced point of view, to experience a primary encounter with Jesus and to dwell within the symbols generated by that encounter is to find the truth that sets all people free.

But on the way to becoming a believer, something else may happen. The primary encounter with Jesus may suddenly take a different direction. At the same time that it is creating life-giving convictions, it may also create the desire to know more about the person of Jesus. We may find ourselves on the roads of Palestine wondering how we got there. The glorious truths of Christian faith are incarnated in a man who called himself a sweet yoke and a light burden. And we may find ourselves trying on that yoke and shouldering that burden. That is the "something else" this book is about.

Perhaps the best way to begin is by noticing something that often goes unnoticed. An inescapable part of our lives is apprenticing ourselves to others. This is obviously true in childhood when we are in a continual learning posture. Our parents teach us everything from how to walk to how to talk to how to eat. We become who we are by apprenticing ourselves to them.

But this process of learning through watching others continues beyond childhood. We find our models in the teenage years, our mentors in the middle years, and our examples of graciousness in the senior years. We find in other people possibilities of living for ourselves. And, lo and behold, when we turn around, we notice other people are apprenticing themselves to us at

the same time that we are apprenticing ourselves to others. It is a circle, not vicious, but interdependent and unavoidable in the huddled human condition.

Part One of this book develops this modeling, mentoring, mastering process which is essential to interdependent human life. Chapter One suggests that we apprentice ourselves to people whom we find fascinating. And what we find fascinating about them is their liberating responses to the situations which confront them. We want to know how to respond in similar ways, but we also want to find the underlying power that makes possible these liberating responses. Both the response and the power of the response intrigue us.

This natural human dynamic is our entry into the Jesus story. The people we apprentice ourselves to as "masters" themselves have a Master. They introduce us to Jesus. He the One who taught them how to live and die in the way we find so appealing. But when we approach Jesus, we must get beyond his reputation. We ourselves must find him fascinating. This is the project which occupies Chapter Two and Chapter Three, and if it is carried through to its conclusion, it results in discipleship.

Part Two of the book develops the ins and outs of discipleship to Jesus. Naming Jesus the Spirit Master means we bring our concerns about the human spirit to him for acceptance, transformation, and hope. This is a rigorous process, and the more we understand it, the more fully we are able to participate in it. If we knock on the door of Jesus, we must be ready if he opens it. The ones who seek must be prepared to find; the ones who ask must brace themselves to receive. Chapter Four tries to spell out the underlying presuppositions of a master-disciple relationship.

In our time, the major resource for apprenticing ourselves to Jesus is the Gospels. Therefore, we must spend time with the stories of Jesus and understand his art, the way he trains people to see and hear what he sees and hears. We must also watch him at work and see if he can train us while he is training others. Chapter Five and Chapter Six will initiate us into this way of third-party discipleship.

Part Three of our exploration will be friendship. We will have moved from fascination through discipleship to arrive at friendship. But friendship does not mean that fascination and discipleship are abandoned. Just the opposite: fascination and discipleship are permanent aspects of friendship with Jesus. Jesus himself defines the terms of friendship:

> I no longer speak of you as slaves,
> for a slave does not know what his
> master is about.
> Instead, I call you friends,
> since I have made known to you all
> that I heard from my Father.
>
> John 15:15

If discipleship is successful and we find the power that Jesus calls "Abba," then the dynamics of friendship begin. To be a friend of Jesus is to have a share in his identity and mission.

Part One and Part Two on fascination and discipleship are written in a standard expository way. Part Three on friendship takes a different track. When the disciple learns from the Master his way of life, the disciple may respond in many different ways. The premier response is action; the disciple embodies the way of the Master. But the disciple may also respond through reflective thought and imagination. The section on friendship is a response through imagination. I attempt to take the insights which the inspired imagination of

Scripture has triggered in me and recast them in stories. Hopefully, some wisdom about the way of Jesus emerges in the juxtaposition of that inspired imagination and the creations of my answering imagination.

Whoever said "No book is ever finished; the author just stops writing" has accurately summed up my feelings. The considerations on fascination, discipleship, and friendship need further elaboration, and by all rights, there could be a fourth part to this book. Love brings to fulfillment the spiritual movements embodied in fascination, discipleship, and friendship. As the opening quotation from Karl Rahner suggests, we should be able to throw our arms around Jesus. This is *not* a book about throwing our arms around Jesus. This is a book about getting to know him well enough that we might *want* to throw our arms round him.

In Rahner's excellent chapter on "Love for Jesus" he stresses that the fact that Jesus is cut off from us by "geographical space, by the distance of history and culture, and by the span of two thousand years" does not mean we are reduced to loving only a "Christ-idea."[5] We can have a real relationship with the concrete, radical person of Jesus of Nazareth. Rahner gives hints on how this real relationship is possible. This is encouraging, for if we know the possibility is there, we will be alert. The possible may become the actual. But there is another problem about throwing our arms around Jesus.

Is he all that huggable?

I have heard people tell how they have embraced Jesus, and I could not hold back the suspicion that they were embracing only themselves. I was at a baptism where someone prayed that the child would be a friend of Jesus. I thought to myself, "That is a very dangerous prayer." A student asked me if I had a personal relationship with Jesus. I said yes. He said he did, too, and wasn't it wonderful? I could not quite say my relationship to Jesus over the years has been wonderful.

I mention these thoughts to reveal the spiritual sensitivity or lack of it which permeates these pages. For me, the Incarnate Son of God is a "hard" man. He is more grace than we want and more demand than we can handle. I mentioned this to a friend of mine who quickly shot back, "Well, if that's the case, I'm going back to Mary." Once a Catholic, always a Catholic. If I was going to paint a stern portrait and put a scowl on Jesus' face, then he knew where he could find compassion and care. When Jesus shuts the door, Mary opens the window.

Of course, Jesus is not stern, and scowls are only for those who try to intimidate. Jesus is love clear through the middle, and that is the problem. There is no lie in his love and there is no darkness in his light. As St. John suggests, to the degree that we love the truth, we open our ears, and to the degree that we love the light, we open our eyes. But the fact is that to some degree we feed on the lie and hide in the dark. Therefore, our arms stay at our side even though the arms of Jesus are stretched out in welcome.

Perhaps the way to this eventual embrace of Jesus is best stated by Karl Rahner. He opened this Preface; it is only appropriate that he close it.

> It happens that this immediate love for Jesus . . . is not present from the start. It must grow and ripen. The tender interiority of this love, to which it need not be afraid to admit, is the fruit of patience, prayer, and an ever renewed immersion in Scripture. It is the gift of God's Spirit. We cannot commandeer it, we cannot seize it violently and without discretion. But we may always know that the very aspiration to such love is already its beginning, and that we have a promise of its fulfillment.[6]

There are many people to thank for their help in putting together this book—Rita, who edited and corrected as the text emerged and Joel Wells and William Herr, who painstakingly pointed to the flaws of language and punctuation. Then there is more "spread-out" gratitude for all the people who provided support and encouragement. These are my family and friends, and this book is dedicated to them. They know the truth of Rahner's insight that the very aspiration to love is its beginning and that we already have the promise of fulfillment.

PART ONE

FASCINATION

CHAPTER ONE

FAITH AND FASCINATION

Through this wordless witness these Christians stir up irresistible questions in the hearts of those who see how they live: Why are they like this? Why do they live in this way? What or who is it that inspires them? Why are they in our midst? Such a witness is already a silent proclamation of the Good News and a very powerful and effective one.[1]

Pope Paul VI

A story of faith transmission from laughing adults to a solemn kid: If memory serves me well—and it seldom docs—I was in eighth grade when the large black letters on the marquee of the local movie theater announced *Baby Doll,* starring Carroll Baker, was sizzling sex on celluloid. A definite yawn by today's standards, it promised thirteen-year-old boys of the reticent fifties unimaginable sights and secrets. Almost thirty years later, Carroll Baker would entitle her autobiography *Baby Doll* and make us all remember the hubbub.

But I also remember it was a time my fledgling faith caught a glimpse of eagles.

In the small, enclosed Catholic community in which I lived (too humane and loving to bear the connotations of ghetto) *Baby Doll* brought out the beast. An article in the Church's Sunday Bulletin excoriated the owner of the movie theater and forbade people to see the movie. Each nun in the school took time out from math and geography to rail at this indecency and to suggest that the foundations of Catholic morality were being shaken. Cardinal Spellman nationally denounced the movie, thereby polishing the forbidden fruit.

We did what grammar school kids—even eighth graders who, as everyone knew, ran the school—were supposed to do. We watched and learned by good example. What we saw was the steady, loving-stern adults of our lives visibly unhinged. They were angry, outraged, and threatening. And although we nodded, we were not all that sure what precisely it was that was unleashing this fury. Or if fury is too strong a word, this not-to-be-taken-lightly case of ruffled Catholic feathers.

One day a group of us were hanging out in the church parking lot by the basketball courts. The parish priest walked over from the rectory and joined us. Somehow the conversation got onto *Baby Doll.* The parish priest said, 'Yeah, I saw it."

Whenever I hear the word *dumbfounded,* I always remember that long ago day when my mouth fell open, speechless.

"And it's as bad as they say it is," he continued. Then he laughed.

I hustled home (good basketball players always hustle) and told my parents what the priest said. They both laughed. I asked them what they were laughing at.

"How was the basketball game?" said my father, who, following the example of Jesus, always answered a question with a question.

* * *

In contemporary Catholic conversation, the complexities of faith transmission are evoked by a code word: *evangelization.* Evangelization was once clearly defined as the preaching of the Gospels that preceded and evoked people's faith response. It was an initiating moment. It still retains that meaning but has been enlarged to include "the activity whereby the Church proclaims the Gospel so that faith may be aroused, may unfold, and may grow."[2] Evangelization is an ongoing process of the Christian community and targets all members of that community, those knowledgeable in the ways of the Lord and those barely beyond ignorance.

The implication of this seems to be that it is the total life of the people which communicates faith. People pass on faith in strange and mysterious ways. It is not merely a communication from older to younger or from clergy to lay or from catechist to catechumen. The mouths of babes may speak the truth to theologians; the ministered unto may build up the faith of the minister; the neophyte may instruct the instructor. Also, it is not restricted to religion classes, Church services, or R. C. I. A. (Rite of Christian Initiation for Adults) processes. Wherever Christians gather—on basketball courts and in kitchens, at parties and at wakes—there exists the possibility that the attitudes, outlooks, and actions of faith might be exchanged.

The suggestion is that the Christian people are Christian in all contexts, perhaps not explicitly Christian but Christian nonetheless. Therefore, in their concrete living, in the give and take of their mutually interacting relationships, part of the communication flow may be faith-inspired attitudes, outlooks, and actions.

This assertion is not merely a romantic democratizing of faith, nor is it meant to so universalize faith transmission that it cannot be distinguished from ordinary conversation and activity. But it is the recognition that life is larger than any imposed institutional order. Actual life is always more than the forms that seek to structure it. Therefore, the way faith is communicated cannot be rigorously restricted to sanctioned channels.

But there is a need for structure. The drive to pass on Christian faith is not an external obligation. It arises from the heart of a faith whose wisdom suggests that you can hold onto only what you give away. And the possibilities of giving faith away increase when we put some order into the offer.

In *Evangelii Nuntiandi,* Paul VI enumerates seven elements in the evangelization process: (1) renewal of humanity, (2) Christian witness, (3) explicit proclamation of the Word, (4) inner adherence, (5) entrance into the community, (6) acceptance of signs, and (7) apostolic initiative.[3] The document does not attempt a logical or developmental sequence to these elements. This is just as well. Different programs put them together in different ways based on the sensibilities of the people, the cultural and political atmosphere, and the resources of the local church.[4]

But even after the programs of lifelong evangelization are firmly in place, the messiness and unpredictability of informal faith communication continue to go on. These two dimensions of faith communication—the formal and the informal, the structured and the unstructured—are not competitors. They interact and complement one another.

But our concern, at least at the beginning, will be informal faith communication, a type of transmission that goes on among Christians but which often escapes notice. We will not explore it with the ambition of translating its dynamics into a program, but merely because this may be part of our lives and it would be good to recognize it.

A story of faith transmission from a suffering woman to a watching woman: About thirty people gathered for the post-funeral luncheon. Joe, a relatively young man, had died of cancer. Throughout his illness, his wife, Nan, was present to him in ways so realistic yet so loving that we all took notice. A neighbor lady (Chicagoese for good friend on the block) came up to me and said, "I hope this doesn't sound morbid, and God forbid it should ever happen. But if it does, I hope I can be there for Pete [her husband] the way Nan was there for Joe."

* * *

Our exploration of the informal dynamics of faith transmission will be partially descriptive and partially prescriptive. It will be descriptive in the sense that it attempts to make explicit what has happened and what is happening. I believe this process is partially how faith was nurtured and still is nurtured in me, and in listening to other people, it is also a part of their continuing faith history. The two stories which I have related capture moments of informal faith transmission. The priest and my parents passed on faith to me through their responses to *Baby Doll,* and the "watching woman" received an invitation to faith from the "suffering woman." This type of transmission often happens quickly and through language and action which we do not immediately associate as religious.

This form of faith transmission is prescriptive in that its dynamics may well increase in the future. The reason for this is that it taps into some of the inbred values of the secular culture. It stresses interpersonal relationships, action, freedom, and personal experience. But most of all, it holds together the framework of faith in a way that is accessible to secular people.

The framework of faith is the relationship to God (the vertical dimension) and neighbor (the horizontal dimension). These two dimensions can be distinguished but not separated. The usual rendition of how they are related stresses the dependency of love of neighbor on love of God. The logic runs: We have an intimate relationship to God, a relationship which was initiated by divine love but which is co-constituted by our response. When our response is full, it flows back to the initiating God in prayer and worship and outward toward our neighbor in compassion and service. But the secret energy of faith is the sustaining power of the relationship to God.

But another way of exploring this double relationship is to observe how it appears within the flow of experience. This logic runs: What we immediately experience are the attitudes, outlooks, and actions of people toward one another and toward their situations. People relating to people, the faith relationship toward neighbor, is what is observable. If these attitudes, outlooks, and actions are of a particular quality, we judge they must be supported and encouraged from a relationship with a deeper reality.

But this deeper relationship is for the most part private, unavailable to everyone but the person involved. We may catch him or her at prayer, but we cannot eavesdrop on the interior dialogue. Our access to a person's faith in God comes mainly from his or her faith relationship toward us, the neighbor. We surmise a relationship to God because of the quality of the relationship toward us. We see the relationship to neighbor; we guess at the relationship to God.

This experiential dynamic, from neighbor to God, will be our major approach as we explore the transmission of faith and the training of people in faith. In order to organize our reflections, we will focus on three experiences. The first experience deals solely with the horizontal dimension of faith, our relationship to our neighbor. It focuses on momentary encounters that prove fascinating, and it leads us, if we follow the lure, to apprenticing ourselves to these fascinating responses.

The second experience unites the horizontal dimension of faith with the vertical. It focuses on long-lasting encounters with fascinating people which lead us, if everything goes right, to apprenticing ourselves to the energizing power of their liberated lives. This energizing power is the reality of God. We will explore these two experiences in this chapter.

The rest of the book will unfold the third experience. This is an everlasting encounter with Jesus Christ. Jesus Christ deepens our relationship to God and extends the relationship to neighbor. The encounter with him is very complex. It leads us, if we dare, to a permanent discipleship and apprenticing ourselves to the power he calls "Abba." If all goes well, the result is friendship with Christ, love of God and neighbor, and the continuance of the Christian way of life.

Momentary Encounters, Fascination, and Faith

If momentary encounters are to stir up a faith response in us, they must be fascinating. We must be attracted to what we see, and if our fascination is to be related to faith, it must be on the level of the "human." We may be intrigued by how restaurateurs become millionaires or how prolific authors write so many books or what whiskey jockeys drink or where sailors sleep in submarines. This is curiosity.

But the fascination that is related to faith has to do with how to live. Sometimes a person's attitudes, outlooks, and actions reveal a mode of being human. What emerges through the concrete nitty-gritty of a situation is a personal and pervasive quality of spirit, a way of being alive that has immediate appeal.

In the two encounters we have related, someone is becoming fascinated with the quality of response that is given in a situation. These are ordinary incidents which stress the "everydayness" of this form of faith communication. Martin Lang distinguishes impressive and landmark experiences.[5] Impressive experiences do just that—they make an impression.

Landmark experiences precipitate a major adjustment or enlightenment. In relation to faith, the experiences which are usually cited are landmark moments, major mystical or conversion events. Our "trigger" encounters are the less powerful but more available impressive experiences. We can use these everyday stories to unravel the dynamics of fascination.

First, fascinating attitudes, outlooks, and actions usually display a different caliber of response to commonly shared situations. This response often contrasts with the expected response or the response of the majority. In short, it stands out. In an atmosphere charged with anger and outrage of other adults, the priest and my parents laughed. This intrigued me, and even at thirteen, I knew this attitude was more creative and life-giving than what was all around me. The suffering woman is in a situation which can reduce people to anger, paralysis, and numbness. Yet she displayed, with uncanny timing and sensitivity, a range of opposite responses—from action to acceptance to mutual loss.

Second, a response appears fascinating because we find it liberating. There are objective and subjective sides to a liberating response. Objectively, a response is liberating when it modifies the human condition in the direction of redemption. This modification may affect many people, as in the signing of a peace treaty, or it may be one of the "small kindnesses," the reaching out of a hand to a person who has fallen. But whenever the human condition is saved, however briefly, from the powers that threatened it, those actions are liberating.

Subjectively, a response is liberating when it shows us a possibility of thinking, feeling, and acting which, at the present moment, we are not capable of but which we wish we were capable of. "Stuff we know" may be objectively liberating, but it is the "stuff we don't know" that is both liberating and fascinating. This means that it is not completely beyond us and yet it is not completely within our reach. The actions, attitudes, or outlooks which fascinate us fall somewhere between "totally weird" and "completely understandable." They relate to where we are at and provide a glimpse of where we could be.

In those long ago years, I felt vaguely uncomfortable in an environment of anger sharing an anger which I did not fully understand. But I knew no other response until I saw it in the priest and my parents. What I saw was that humor was a possible alternative to outrage. I was not sure how it worked, but I knew that life was better laughing at *Baby Doll* than shouting at it. The "watching woman" saw in the "suffering woman" a liberating way of responding to tragedy. Although we do not know, she probably could not have managed such a creatively human response on her own. But once she saw it, she knew it.

Third, fascinating responses can create in us a variety of reactions. We will consider two spontaneous feelings—astonishment and desire. They often overlap and interact with one another. But they can also be separated. We can feel astonished by a fascinating response but not feel a desire to pursue its possibilities for our own lives. When desire is aroused in us, it is because the response has claimed us. What we saw and heard had our "name" on it.

When we are astonished, the emphasis in our reaction is on praising what has just occurred. What we have seen and heard we consider remarkable, and we exclaim our wonder in ways that range from applause to shouting. There is a biblical parallel to this process. When people saw Jesus respond to situations, they were astonished (Mt. 12:23; 15:31; Mk. 5:42; Lk. 8:56). This astonishment led them to praise God. Their fascination with what happened was so great that their appreciation did not stop at Jesus. It moved to the source of life itself which was somehow involved and whose values were revealed and promoted. There was astonishment present in both the *Baby Doll* and "watching woman" incidents, but no praise of divine power burst forth. Most likely it was not the right time or place. But then again, it could be another example of feeling life in a certain way but not being able to express it.

My suggestion is that the richness and variety of life offer us astonishment at every turn. The human situation is being modified in the direction of redemption daily. We are witnesses to this. I have seen a mother lean down to correct a child and say words so perfect, say sentences of such loving discipline, that, if the truth of what is happening is to be known, God must be praised. I have seen a man face death in such a way that it had no sting, and my astonishment made me mute. I listened to a woman forgive a system that had badly violated her and forgive the men and women in that system who were the victims of its influence. She forgave them not because she was too weak to retaliate but because forgiveness was the only way life could be served, both in her and in those who had hurt her.

People, ordinary and extraordinary, are daily leaning into life and either coaxing or muscling it toward redemption. If we catch them at it and find ourselves once more astonished, we might say "Yes!" and that yes will reach all the way to whatever reality prompted both their fascinating action and our wholehearted appreciation.

The Gospels often picture people "going away" praising God, and this is often the way of astonishment. It is a response of praise, and more often than not, it stops there. It does not feel any personal draw to the fascinating response that provoked it. What happened was wonderful and will not be forgotten, but there was little or no allure. The claim is missing.

But for some people, astonishment mixes with desire. What happened is a magnet; it draws them. When we are drawn to a fascinating response, we feel a desire to make the response, in some way, our own. It is in the drawing process that faith is not only seen and praised but also transmitted. The claim is present.

When we feel desire, we apprentice ourselves to the fascinating response. We do this by remembering the encounter, thinking about it, talking about it, testing out its wisdom, and in general, trying to make it part of ourselves. In the light of our stories we say things like "I'm going to try not to let anger overcome me" or "I'm going to try not to be so standoffish when it comes to sickness." Apprenticing ourselves to the response entails accepting its critique of where we are at and accepting its offer to try something new. In this sense, the encounter with a fascinating attitude, outlook, or action is only the beginning. If it is to have any sustained impact, it must live on in reflection, conversation, and actual application.

Of course, most of the momentary encounters which prove fascinating happen and are gone. They fall into forgetfulness. This is probably the natural way of things. But if that is the fate of all our possible faith-enriching encounters, we go through life uninformed by the events we have undergone. If we pursue nothing that modifies the human situation in the direction of redemption and attracts us into a new way of being with our neighbor, perhaps we had better hear again the parable of the sower and seed (Mk. 4:1–20).

In the first telling of the parable (Mk. 4:3–9), the emphasis is on the searching seed. It lands on footpaths, rocky soil, and thorns. None of these nurtures it. Finally, it finds good ground which receives it and produces a harvest. This reading stresses divine persistence and gives us a reason for hope. We may reject the invitations which fascinating responses offer us, but the Source of Life in its infinite prodigality will continue the shower of seed.

The second telling of the parable (Mk. 4:14–20), emphasizes the diversity of soils. The seed has intense competition.

The birds who carry it away are Satan. The rocky ground represents the rootless people who hear the invitation and say yes, but do not carry through. The thorns are those who are preoccupied with anxiety over life's demands and the desire for wealth. The good soil presents those who listen and take it to heart. The seed is everywhere, but no one knows what reception it will receive. These two tellings combine to uncover a dialogic pattern of faith. Faith is a persistent offer which we can either accept or refuse.

Faith in the Second or New Testament is always an invitation that demands a decision. But when we heighten our sensitivity to the dynamics of faith and fascination, this decision-making aspect takes on a new meaning. In the first moment, it may not be a christological decision about whether Jesus is God's Son. It may be the more mundane decision of whether we will pursue what we find fascinating or continue with business as usual.

As the parable of the Great Supper highlights, the most common of all noes is "I have something else to do." Or, as Woody Allen once observed, they discovered a primitive tribe whose vocabulary did not have a word for no. Instead, they said, "I'll get back to you later." In other words, if faith is to be transmitted, we must imitate Moses and turn aside to see a great sight (Ex. 3:3).

But there is one type of refusal that deserves special attention. This refusal is not a turning away to other lesser pursuits, but a turning toward the fascinating response in envy. Envy does not simply avoid the invitation; it seeks to undercut it. Envy is drawn to the fascinating response, but it does not feel empowered by it. When envy overtakes us, we feel diminished by the liberating power of other people. We judge the response well beyond what we are capable of, but we are too attracted to walk away. Yet its judgment on us is painful. So we denigrate or ridicule what we secretly find fascinating.

This undercutting is usually socially acceptable and very high sounding. Envy always masks itself. The secret source of envy is a sense of unworthiness that is almost unbearable. To admit to it is very painful. But to engage in necessary criticism is very principled and a worthy disguise. So envy might sound like: "That priest and Shea's parents missed the point. They really don't understand what is involved . . . " "That suffering woman neglected her children, was too confronting toward her husband, should have cried more. . . . " We have all been in those conversations, both as participants and as observers.

Now the crucial thing about envy is that in an abstract way its observations may be true. Perhaps my parents and the priest should have taken *Baby Doll* more seriously. Perhaps the suffering woman suffered all the lacks they say she did. But concretely, these criticisms are not advanced in the interest of completeness. They are functioning to undercut a response which judges us and which we want to neutralize.

Any response which is fascinating enough to transmit faith must be powerful enough to elicit envious rejection. We cannot understand the response of Jesus' contemporaries to him by merely citing that some accepted him and some walked away. Some kept in touch with murderous intent. The ultimate strategy of envy is to punish the person whose responses to life we find so liberating that the quality of our own life comes under judgment.

Our previous suggestion was that if we have the eyes and ears, fascinating encounters which have the power to cause astonishment abound. The further suggestion is that some of these abundant encounters may attract us to such an extent that we apprentice ourselves to them. It should be noted that at this stage in the process it is not the people, in and of themselves, who fascinate us. It is their actions, attitudes, and outlooks which lure us, and it is those which we attempt to appropriate.

We are not talking about saints, but about flawed people who, in this one situation and for this limited period of time, startle us. Flannery O'Connor once wrote, "The trees were full of silver-white sunlight, and even the meanest of them sparkled."[6] So it is with us. At the right time and place, even the meanest of us become fascinating.

Long-lasting Encounters, Fascination and Faith

The seminarians called the spiritual director I chose "a man of God." It was a fifty percent mock. In 1964, it was very difficult to get away with being a man of God.

For two years I saw him on a daily basis around the seminary and for a formal conference every two weeks. We kept in touch for a few years after my ordination. A year ago I received in the mail a black bordered card with his picture on it. The dates of his life were printed below his picture.

Once I went to see him with a poem I was working on, an epic poem no less, an epic poem in iambic pentameter no less—ah, ambition. He said some of the images were good but what was best about it was that he learned more about me and where I was at. He was always honest to his "reckoning," no more and no less.

Another time I went to see him with a complaint about something that was happening in the seminary. I felt the faculty was being unjust and secretly punishing a student for asking questions in class. When I was done presenting my evidence, I shrugged my shoulders. "I guess there is not much we can do." He pushed himself out of his chair. "There certainly is," he said, as he left the room.

After he had recovered from his first heart attack, we went out to dinner. I asked how it happened. He said he was coming out of the bathroom when an elephant stepped on his chest. He naturally laid down. When the intense pain receded, he reached for the phone and called the doctor who immediately sent an ambulance. Then, risking a second seizure, he put on his robe.

* * *

In the course of life, we run into many responses that sparkle. Also, if we are fortunate, we come into contact with people who radiate on a regular basis. Some people display a whole range of fascinating responses to many different situations. They modify the human condition in the direction of redemption both at work and in the home, in political action and religious practice, in hospitality and confrontation, in the laziness of a Sunday afternoon park or in the heat and shout of a town hall. They seem to be wise "across the board." They know the secrets of money, sex, ambition, work, and love. In our eyes, they know how to live.

We make these people, who appear permanently fascinating to us, our masters. We apprentice ourselves to them, usually in a sly and anonymous fashion, to see if we can learn what they know. My spiritual director taught me how to say no more or no less than I thought, not to construe situations in such a way that there is nothing that can be done, and (something I have not learned well) a bewildering sense of propriety. Long-lasting encounters entail a series of fascinating responses and so communicate the horizontal dimension of faith toward neighbor in a diversified and ongoing way.

But in long-lasting relationships, more becomes evident than in momentary encounters. We begin to surmise that these fascinating responses are possible because the person is working out of a vision of life which is creative and adaptive.

What we gradually become aware of is the vision which guides the actions. Even deeper than that, we suspect that the capacity to respond comes from some power the person is in touch with. They do not so much possess their own response as participate in a power which engenders their liberating responses. If they introduce us to this power of response, they go beyond communicating the horizontal dimension of faith toward neighbor. They open up for us the vertical dimension of faith toward God. God is the source of the liberating responses toward neighbor.

A parable teaches this movement from fascinating responses toward neighbor to contact with the divine power of response:

> The sannyasi had reached the outskirts of the village and settled down under a tree for the night when a villager came running up to him and said, "The stone! The stone! Give me the precious stone!"
>
> "What stone?" asked the sannyasi.
>
> "Last night the Lord Shiva appeared to me in a dream," said the villager, "and told me that if I went to the outskirts of the village at dusk I should find a sannyasi who would give me a precious stone that would make me rich forever."
>
> The sannyasi rummaged in his bag and pulled out a stone. "He probably meant this," he said, as he handed the stone over to the villager. "I found it on a forest path some days ago. You can certainly have it."
>
> The man looked at the stone in wonder. It was a diamond. Probably the largest diamond in the whole world for it was as large as a man's head.

> He took the diamond and walked away. All night he tossed about in bed, unable to sleep. Next day at the crack of dawn he woke the sannyasi and said, "Give me the wealth that makes it possible for you to give this diamond away so easily."[7]

If we are true religious seekers, we are never fully satisfied with the surface of events. The movements on the surface are because of some agitation in the depths. What we want is not some diamond, but the power to give and receive diamonds. We want to know "where the sannyasi lives" because where he lives is the source of what he is able to do. It is this source that we wish to contact. It is the crucial and classic difference between being given a fish and learning how to fish.

In our culture, explicit master-disciple relationships are rare. But what is fairly common is a master-disciple dimension to our long lasting relationships. In long-lasting relationships—parent-child, brother-sister, brother-brother, sister-sister, teacher-student, husband-wife, mentor-mentee, friend-friend—there exists an ongoing fascination with the other's ability to respond to life. It is for this reason that we continually consult each other as we make our decisions. Who is the master and who is the disciple alternates, and as long as the relationship is reciprocal, who is teaching and who is learning is not a matter of great importance. What is important is to live in such a way that existence is modified in the direction of redemption.

These long-lasting relationships which have a master-disciple dimension change considerably with the passage of time. At times, the master-disciple dimension of the relationship is prominent; at other times, it is dormant.

Our parents are the first masters of faith transmission, showing us how to live in the differing situations of life and introducing us into the power to live that way. As such there may be a permanent master-disciple dimension to the parent-child relationship. More likely than not, that dimension of the relationship will fade, but the relationship itself will flourish on other terms.

The same may be true for those who showed us how to live as teens. They may still be our friends, but the master-disciple dimension of that friendship may be relatively inactive. We live in multiple and serial master-disciple relationships.

Alice Walker's novel *The Color Purple* has a wonderful example of a friendship with a strong master-disciple accent. Celie is a depressed and battered woman who is fascinated by the free-wheeling style of Shug Avery, a sometime lover of her husband. Celie falls in love with Shug, and Shug takes her, not under her wings, but on her wings to show her how to fly. She shows her new ways to respond to the situations that oppress her. But one day, in a long conversation about God, she introduces her to the power of her own liberation.

> Here's the thing, say Shug. The thing I believe. God is inside you and inside everybody else. You come into the world with God. But only them that search for it inside find it. And sometimes it just manifest itself even if you not looking, or don't know what you looking for . . .
>
> It? I ast.
>
> Yeah, It. God ain't a he or she, but an It.
>
> But what do it look like? I ast.
>
> Don't look like nothing, she say. It ain't a picture show. It ain't something you can look at apart from anything else, including yourself. I believe God is everything, say Shug. Everything that is or ever was

> or ever will be. And when you can feel that, and be happy to feel that, you've found it . . .
>
> Listen, God love everything you love—and a mess of stuff you don't. But more than anything else God love admiration.
>
> You say God vain? I ast.
>
> Naw, she says. Not vain, just want to share a good thing. I think it pisses God off if you walk by the color purple in a field somewhere and don't notice it.
>
> What it do when it pissed off? I ast.
>
> Oh, it make something else. People think pleasing God is all God care about. But any fool living in the world can see it always trying to please us back . . . It always making little surprises and springing them on us when us least expect.
>
> You mean it want to be loved, just like the Bible say.
>
> Yes, Celie, she say. Everything want to be loved. Us sing and dance, make faces and give flower bouquets, trying to be loved. You ever notice that trees do everything to git attention we do, except walk?[8]

When Celie finally tells off her husband, she writes. "I give it to him straight, just like it come to me. And it seem to come to me from the trees." Shug is a full master. She has taken a fascinated disciple and introduced her to the power of her own liberation. Once Celie is introduced to this power, she begins to live out of it.

There are weaknesses and strengths in this way of apprenticeship. One obvious weakness is that the communication of faith is implicit. Often the master-disciple relationship is not acknowledged, or even if it is, it is not structured. The disciple is too much on his or her own, and the learnings are too sporadic. There is not a scheduled time for encouragement and correction. Encouragement and correction are central to growth in the spirit, and if there is not a disciplined way of doing this, miscommunication is inevitable. When we apprentice ourselves to Jesus, we must find a more consistent and rigorous style of interaction.

A second weakness is that the master-friend may be skilled in living out of the power that he or she participates in but relatively unskilled in passing that power along to others. Not all are as patient and as clever as Shug Avery. They may not understand their roles as masters and might attempt to turn a temporary disciple into a permanent sycophant. They may relate to the disciple in such a way that their own power is secured and the disciple's power is diminished. This perverts the whole process of faith transmission.

My spiritual director had no need to establish himself at my expense. He rested easily in what he knew. He did not grasp the secret energy of his life, so it flowed through him effortlessly and was easily available to me. I lost touch with him and he with me for many years. I remembered him when I came across some remarks on the true and false religious masters.

> After an extended and fruitless search, characterized by many disappointments and "crashing pedestals," when I least expected it, but most needed it, I met the first genuine mystic and, through her, three or four others. Recognizing a profound kinship with such people and also that they knew and had realized far more than I, I set

> upon seeking to unfold within myself what I recognized and admired in them. Their most unanimous and persistent warning, however, was that they could not "teach me" or "give me" what I hungered for, but merely "point the way" to what I should do to unfold spiritual consciousness in myself.[9]

People who have the capacity to communicate faith in God are those who know they can only "point the way." They do not possess the power they have experienced and which has expressed itself through them.

There are also some strengths in this multiple and serial type of master-disciple relationships. When many people function as masters in our lives, we know the power of response is wider than the people involved. There is little chance of absolutizing a particular guru. Also, we are introduced to the power of God under different valences. I have, through many momentary masters, met the source of liberating responses as the power of infinite protest; the power to pursue the stimulating without fear; the power to care in the face of indifference; the power to keep the mind humble as its capacities increase; and the power to attend, without distraction, to each person met. Introductions to God are always extended under the names we know her by. More names, greater knowledge.

Another advantage to multiple and serial masters is that their nonpermanent status clears the way for Christ. The presence of Christ as the permanent Master does not do away with the need for contemporary masters. Momentary and long-lasting encounters continue to mediate faith, but they are not absolutized. They point beyond themselves. When Christians function as guides into the double relationship of faith, they are reflecting the "pioneer and perfecter" of faith (Heb. 12:2). And when contemporary Christian masters have sufficient self-knowledge, they know what their task is. They are to join the long line of people who have passed along the good news. They are to introduce others to the one who has introduced them to the power they know as "Abba." We must meet Jesus.

CHAPTER TWO

FASCINATION WITH JESUS: BIRTH AND RESURRECTION

Q. When did you first hear about Jesus?
A. The first thing I remember about my childhood . . . is the enormous crib that we had at home every Christmas . . . My mother had a fine alto voice and used to sing carols. She sang wonderfully. I think that was why Christmas and the crib appealed so much to me as a child. And then, of course, there were all those human figures and, well, there is God—that baby is God! In so far as I remember it correctly, all that appealed to me![1]

Edward Schillebeeckx

An artist, at first only painfully aware of an utter emptiness and impotence, finds his imagination gradually stirred into life and discovers a vision which takes control of him and which he feels not only able but compelled to express. That is resurrection . . .

Or a married couple find their old relationship, once rich and fulfilling, slowly drying up into no more than an external observance to the point where it seemed impossible that these dry bones should ever live again. Then a new relationship emerges, less superficially high powered and less greedy than the old one, but deeper, more stable, more satisfying, with a new quality of life which is inexhaustible because it does not depend on the constant recharging of emotional batteries. That is resurrection.
Or suffering, a severe illness, or a catastrophe like the premature death of someone deeply loved, such suffering is always destructive. People, we say, are never the same again. Sometimes they shrivel up and atrophy. But

appearances here can be deceptive. Under the devastation of their ordeal which leaves its deep and permanent traces, one can be aware that they are in touch with a new dimension of reality. They have somehow penetrated to the centre of the universe. They are greater people. They are more deeply alive. That is resurrection.[2]

H. A. Williams

If we are to arrive at Jesus, someone must play the role of the woman at the well (Jn. 4:4–42). Someone who has encountered Jesus and through him found a salvific way of living must encourage us. "Come and see someone who told me everything I ever did" is the invitation the woman at the well extends to her fellow villagers. We have suggested that this witnessing role is most effective when played by the people we have apprenticed ourselves to. If they tell us that the torch they hold was lit from the fire of Christ, we eagerly turn to the source. But they are only one voice of a chorus or, to change the metaphor, a single cumulus in clouds of witnesses (Heb. 12:1). In reality, it is the entire Christian tradition which, in all its glory and folly, points to Christ as the source of its virtue and the inspiration of its repentance.

But still this remains the testimony of others. There must also be our own appraisal. "Could not this be the Messiah?" is the tentative suggestion of the woman at the well. With that possibility in mind, the villagers beg Jesus to stay with them. When he leaves, they tell the woman, "No longer does our faith depend on your story. We have heard for ourselves, and we know that this really is the Savior of the world." This is the full communication of faith—from receiving a witness to encountering the reality which is witnessed to.

The Jesus we are introduced to must pass the test of personal fascination. It is not enough to take the word of another or even the word of a tradition as ancient and venerable as Christianity. We must be able to say for ourselves, "He told me everything I ever did." If the Jesus story is to be ever new, we must find in it an attraction strong enough to compete with all the other attractions which vie for our allegiance. There never was a time when Jesus was not in the marketplace, and today he is in the marketplace more than ever. He stands side by side with other images of the truly human and masters of authentic living. His power to save begins with his power to attract. If we are to seriously consider apprenticing ourselves to him, his story must be powerful enough to claim our attention.

In other words, Jesus' exalted role in Christian faith does not exempt him from the task of attracting each generation anew. When we come into contact with his story, we must experience that blend of elements that make for fascination. We suggested that what fascinates us must contrast with what is normally expected and must appeal to us as personally liberating.

In responding to what we find fascinating, we may express astonishment and let it go at that; or we may feel a claim on us which evokes a desire to know more; or we may experience envy and begin a campaign to discredit what we are attracted to. These elements—contrast, liberation, astonishment, desire, and envy—can come together in an infinite variety of ways.

But for our purposes, we are looking for a fascination with the Jesus story that has the power to claim us and evoke a response of desire. We want to find that something which will compel us to turn aside and consider a deeper relationship. So if some aspect of the Jesus story leaps out and offers us a liberating possibility, we will argue that if part of the story could do that, what might the whole story be able to do? Or if we are astonished at some particular response of Jesus, we will be invited to walk with him a bit further for surely something even greater will happen just down the road. Or if we are in the grip of envy and cynically dismiss something because it overwhelms us, we will be urged to look again with a little less fear and a little more confidence. The goal of fascination is to hear the claim and create the desire. Desire is the beginning of discipleship.

There is a major difference between the dynamics of fascination which we explored in Chapter One and fascination with Jesus. In momentary encounters and long-lasting relationships, we are physically interacting with other people. We see and talk to them, and they see and talk to us. When we come to Jesus, we are primarily dealing with our stories about him, compressed into the phrase "the Jesus story." This difference will dog our reflections, and we will have to respond to it both theologically and practically.

For the moment, a bold statement will suffice: Although we are reading or listening to Jesus' story, we do not timidly say that we are just interacting with his story. We say we are encountering the reality of Jesus mediated through his story. If we are fascinated, it will be he who will be drawing us, and if we apprentice ourselves, it will be to him.

There is a theology about how this is possible.[3] Its essential elements are the presence of Christ through the Spirit to his followers, the presence of Christ in his inspired story, and the interaction between the believers and the story. But our concern is more the actuality of an encounter with Jesus through his story than the construction of the theoretical possibility of such an encounter. We are searching for what in the story makes us stop, look, listen, and consequently meet Jesus.

So what is it in the story of Jesus that is fascinating? What is the initial draw? What will get us to turn aside, to stop business as usual, to take the first step?

My suspicion is that if we listened to all the men and women who have found Jesus irresistible, they would describe different qualities and retell different scriptural episodes. In fact, probably every line of the Gospels has been, at one time or another, a source of fascination for someone. His silence may attract us as much as his words, his retreat to the mountains as much as his entry into the city, the overturned tables as much as the table fellowship, his outbursts at injustice as much as his praise of faith. The history of Christian discipleship suggests that the total gospel story, in all its details, has the power to attract.

One reason for this is that we come to the Jesus story with our own life conflicts uppermost in our minds, and we search for words and actions which will speak to them. As a friend says, for a mother with a sick child the passion narrative is ultimately about sick children. That no one can serve two masters may be the wisdom we need when we are torn apart by competing loyalties. Jesus' simple response to the sight of a crowd—"Where will we get enough food?"—may amaze us when all we are used to is leaders asking, "Have you come to make me King?"

We may find in Jesus' ongoing criticism of those he loves the power we need to introduce challenge into our intimate relationships. Jesus weeping over Jerusalem may free us to weep for all we have deeply desired and not been able to accomplish. What fascinates us usually speaks very concretely to our situation and offers the possibility of modifying it in the direction of redemption.

Therefore, each of us must witness to the attractive power of the story of Jesus and specify, as best we can, what it is that draws us. Every relationship to Jesus that grows and develops follows its own peculiar path. Cardinal Newman stressed this inescapably individual aspect paradoxically.

> In these provinces of inquiry egotism is true modesty . . . in religious inquiry each of us can speak only for himself, and for himself he has a right to speak. His own experiences are enough for himself, but he cannot speak for others: he cannot lay down the law.[4]

When the question is fascination, the abstract and the universal must wait upon the testimony of individual women and men.

However, this primacy of the personal is not a victory for the idiosyncratic. It does not mean we merely "read into" the Gospels our own agenda. Rather, we find or tumble upon a creative match between our own existential concerns and the concerns reflected in the stories. The Gospels reflect definite historical situations in the life of Jesus and the early Church. But many of these situations were appropriated at such a depth that they have transhistorical resonances. They speak to us through the centuries because we are engaged in similar struggles. This is part of the learning in Raymond Brown's comment on the diverse portrayals of the passion of Jesus in the four Gospels.

> There are moments in the lives of most Christians when they need desperately to cry out with the Marcan/Matthean Jesus, "My God, my God, why have you forsaken me?" and to find, as Jesus did, that despite human appearances God is listening and can reverse tragedy. At other moments, meaning in suffering may be linked to being able to say

> with the Lucan Jesus, "Father, forgive them for they know not what they do," and being able to entrust oneself confidently to God's hands. There are still other moments when with Johannine faith we must see that suffering and evil have no real power over God's Son or over those whom he enables to become God's children . . . It is important that some be able to see the head bowed in dejection, while others observe the arms outstretched in forgiveness, and still others perceive in the title on the cross the proclamation of a reigning king.[5]

The actual diversity and richness of the gospel portraits are the objective grounding for their rich and diverse use by contemporary Christians.

But we can complement individual testimony with general patterns of the Jesus story which seem to have wide appeal. We are incorrigibly individual, but we are also disturbingly alike. In theological language, we all participate in created existence and so share the fundamental dynamics that arise out of finitude. Therefore, we approach the Jesus story not only as unique individuals but also as common creatures.

When we do, we encounter a Jesus who is "intensified creation." The normal processes of finite life are focused and heightened in him and in the stories that witness to him. The New Adam in Jesus can speak to the Adam and Eve in every human being (Lk. 3:38; Rm. 5:14). As long as we do not attempt to restrict the multifaceted power of the story, we can select different moments that may have universal appeal and suggest their ability to attract us.

Our suggestion is that the birth of Jesus may fascinate us because it relates to our chronic question about whether we have any worth in a life so fleeting and fickle. We will highlight

Jesus' birth under the title "The Baby Is God." The resurrection of Jesus attracts us because we ask about our status and destiny in the face of all the things that tear us down and destroy us. We will highlight the resurrection of Jesus under the title, "Risen from the Dead." Both of these explorations will lead us to the life and death of Jesus which we will highlight in the next chapter under the title "The One Who Knows How to Live and Die." These would seem to be the logical, if perhaps too large, divisions of the Jesus story. But when we ask how to approach the birth and resurrection narratives, a great deal of complexity surfaces.

First, we must not overlook the fact that these are stories, and although some of the characterization is thin and some of the plots sketchy, they are separately and collectively compelling tales. We may be dulled to their narrative style through overexposure, or we may not hear some of the "explosions" in the text because of theological prejudices or historical distance. But if we defamiliarize ourselves, we will be drawn into the flow of events and find ourselves emotionally involved. These are not slapdash renditions, but ingenious narrative creations which have all the ingredients necessary to grab and hold the reader or listener.

The ability of the birth and resurrection stories to fascinate us presupposes their literary artistry. It is not merely a happy accident that powerful religious stories are also great literature. Their artistry is directly connected to their potential to evoke religious feeling and provoke theological reflection. Divine reality may be able to enter the heart directly, but if it is to get in through the normal channels of eye and ear, it needs a spokesperson or writer. The harsh truth of divine-human cooperation is that unless the stories work as stories, they will not be fully effective on the level of religious communication. It is difficult to hear life-giving truth in a boring story or to engage the complexity of human living out of a simpleminded narrative.

Second, we have four overall stories of Jesus. Each of these stories presents a different picture of Jesus and selects and rearranges episodes for specific purposes. Through a combination of literary and historical approaches, we can uncover some of the original meanings of the four evangelists and the concerns of the early Christian communities.

Some of these original meanings and concerns appear anything but fascinating. They are dated material, historically interesting but not immediately compelling. But other meanings and concerns seem to have immense attractive power. To retrieve some of these original meanings might be to find ourselves, in Paul Ricoeur's phrase, once more astonished.

Third, the stories have been handed on through the centuries by the Christian people, and they have left their fingerprints. The tradition has shaped and reshaped the stories in many ways. The popular tradition has tended to synthesize the four stories into a single narrative. We were told the story of Jesus' birth, not the infancy narratives of Matthew and Luke. We were regaled with the resurrection stories, not the Lukan journey to Emmaus or Matthew's mountaintop commissioning. Although there were four gospels, in the popular mind there was one story.

This single story has a history of preferential interpretation that accompanies it. We came in contact with the Jesus story mediated through the tradition with its accumulated theology and current set of concerns. We read the story with a specific set of theological glasses and heard it with a specific theological hearing aid. We knew that Jesus' birth was the incarnation of the eternal Son of God and that his resurrection conquered death. The stories contained more than these theological perceptions, but these theological perceptions effectively hid whatever that "more" might be.

From the point of view of fascination, this development of combining four stories into one and suffusing it with a single theological meaning was both a blessing and a curse. It was a blessing because the accepted theological reading of the story communicated a meaning which previous generations had found fascinating. It focused attention and readied the reader or listener for clearly identifiable feelings and thoughts.

In doing this, the overriding theology and the community and tradition that carried it turned the infancy narratives into Christmas and the resurrection stories into Easter. These feasts and the interpretation of the stories which are at their center communicate something central to faith and, at least for me, something enduringly fascinating.

The curse is one that is common in the interpretation of narrative. The narrative is primary and capable of generating many interpretations. In the course of time, one interpretation becomes so tightly linked with the narrative that it is difficult to enter the narrative on any terms other than those of the dominant interpretation.

The narrative plus its privileged interpretation become predictable and boring. What was once startling and astonishing becomes an unsurprising rerun. In regard to the Gospels the wag remarks that it may be good but it is no longer news. No sooner do we hear or read the story than we know its meaning. We do not follow its twists and turns and puzzle at its strangeness. Our hair-trigger response is "Oh, that one means God loves you." Yawn.

Our approach to the birth and resurrection stories will be to interrelate these three perspectives. We will try to sensitize ourselves to these stories as stories by noting the characters, their actions, and their predicaments. Hopefully, this exercise will generate interest in these people and what is happening to them. Next, we will engage in some literary and historical analysis to unravel a few of the meanings which these stories originally carried. Finally, we will look at the privileged interpretation attached to these stories. When we hold these three perspectives together, we may "re-appreciate" the fascinating power of these stories.

The Baby is God

We will briefly run through the infancy narratives of Matthew and Luke, mentioning major characters and giving an inkling of plot. The purpose is to refresh our interest, capture our attention, to hear them once again as intriguing stories before we ponder their religious meaning.

Danger pervades Matthew's story of the birth of Jesus. It is an ominous, dream-directed tale with more terror than joy. It begins by unrolling the sacred scroll of genealogy which reveals that Jesus' birth has been part of a plan that began long ago with God calling Abraham out of Haran. All the people of the past lived so that this child could be born. But this child, both in the womb and out of it, is threatened. His only hope is that a man remembers his dreams when he wakes.

Joseph goes to bed to dream. In his dreams, angels come to him with divine advice and warning. His fiancée is pregnant without his help, but a dream calms him with the news that the child is the work of the Holy Spirit. Later, he dreams that the hoofbeats of Herod's horses will soon come to trample the child, and so he flees with Mary and the baby to Egypt. In Egypt he dreams that Herod is dead and so he returns to Israel, only to be warned in another dream that Archelaus, the son of Herod, is alive so he should not return to Judea. He goes to Nazareth in Galilee. Joseph is a stubborn dreamer who enacts in the day what comes to him at night.

There are also astrologers who follow a star which is following a baby. But if they are called wise men, they are not aptly named. They ask Herod, the present king of the Jews, where the newborn king of the Jews is to be found. To no one's surprise, Herod is disturbed. He lets them go in the hope that they will find the baby and provide him with the information he needs. They continue their quest, and the star reappears in the sky. (For the only time in this story we are told someone is happy.) They find the baby, pay him homage, and give him kingly gifts. Then in a dream, they receive a message of true wisdom—go home without returning to Herod.

There is also Herod, a king of deceit and murder. He plots with his advisors, tries to manipulate the astrologers, becomes furious when his plot fails, and sends out killers for the child slaughter. This is the eternal enmity between kings and babies, the viciousness which makes Rachel cry out, inconsolable for all time.

But one child has escaped.

This is the story of the miraculous birth of a long-awaited child. He is guarded by a dreamer, worshipped by stargazers, and hunted by a king. He finally settles in Nazareth and will be called "the Nazarean." Who will this child, who can inspire such protection in Joseph, such awe in the astrologers, and such hatred in Herod, grow up to be? Quickly turn the page; beg the storyteller to go on.

If Matthew's story should be underscored by drumbeats, Luke's story should be accompanied on the lyre. In Luke, marvel follows marvel; we are dazzled and bedazzled. In Luke, angels do not bother with dreams. They appear in broad daylight and in the night skies, and they are as common as flies. Obviously something important is coming down. In the sanctuary of the Lord, the old man Zechariah is surprised by an angel who tells him he is about to be a father of a son by a wife as old as Sarah's laugh. He is struck mute because he thinks biology is the last word. At the birth of his son, he will sing.

Another angel, or perhaps the same one, appears in Nazareth to a virgin and tells her she will bear a son. She says, "How?" He says, "When the Holy Spirit arrives, nothing is impossible." She says, "Yes!" She visits Elizabeth, her cousin and Zechariah's wife, and the two pregnant women dream about their unborn sons. The child in Elizabeth's womb dances, and Mary sings about a God of favor to the poor and consternation to the rich.

Enter Rome. Caesar Augustus orders everyone around for his own purposes and plays into the hands of God. The dutiful Joseph and Mary, filled with promise, journey to Bethlehem. The child is born, wrapped in swaddling clothes, and laid in a manger. There is something about this child that makes it inappropriate for him to stay at an inn where travelers lodge.

Another angel, or perhaps the same one, tells shepherds that their Shepherd has been born and breaks into song with a multitude of heavenly hosts. The shepherds find the child and break into praise. Mary treasures all these things in her heart.

Mary and Joseph bring the baby boy to the Temple. The old man Simeon says that he can die now for he has seen it all. But he warns Mary that a sword through her heart would be the way all hearts would be laid bare. Then the old woman Anna, after seeing the baby, talks to anyone she can find about salvation. When the boy is twelve, the family goes to Jerusalem. He disappears and thinks his parents should understand. They do not. He goes back to Nazareth with them.

The child is the mute, unmoving center of Luke's story. His importance is signaled by what happens to everyone around him. Barren women and virgins conceive; angels direct events; shepherds praise God; an old man and woman are fulfilled; the heart of Mary who treasures these things is promised a sword. These wonders and the last, teasing line of the Temple story—"Jesus, for his part, progressed steadily in wisdom and age and grace before God and men" (Lk. 2:52)—force us to the same question we asked at the conclusion of Matthew's story: "With a birth and childhood like this, who will this boy grow up to be and what will he do?"

Both these infancy narratives work on the level of story. They are wonderful beginnings. They pique interest and point forward to a life that may be filled with even more wonder and danger than his birth. But when we explore them in terms of their religious meaning, they do more than merely point forward. They foreshadow future events and function as introductions into the themes which will haunt the life of Jesus. They follow the tight law of drama that if you pound a nail in the wall in the first act, somebody has to hang herself from it in the third act. The nails that Matthew and Luke pound into the wall in the infancy narrative are well used in the main body of their stories.

To use a different metaphor, the infancy narratives in Matthew and Luke are overtures to the symphony of the life, death, and resurrection of Jesus. They strike notes in a single chord which will be played at length and with many variations throughout the story. It is the common appraisal of scholarship that, although in the Gospels they naturally appear first, the birth narratives were written last. They are theological reflections in story form on the themes and truths that the life of Jesus revealed. When what was written last is placed first, it has the effect of alerting the reader or listener about what is to come. Some examples will help us explore this process.

The four women of Matthew's genealogy—Tamar, Rahab, Ruth, and the wife of Uriah—are all, to use John Irving's phrase, "sexually suspect." They have all been involved in carrying on the messianic line but in ways that are seemingly scandalous. They prepare us for the scandal of Jesus' birth and, more significantly, for a life and death that is shocking to conventional standards.

In Matthew's account, Mary's pregnancy "before they lived together" immediately throws Joseph into a quandary. Should he "expose her to the law" or should he find some other way which is more in line with the fact that he is an upright man? When we first hear of Jesus, even in the womb, he is forcing a decision. He is embryonic trouble, and the trouble he causes revolves around the tension between what the law prescribes and what love demands. This tension will be at the center of many of his life conflicts.

Matthew's portrait of Herod foreshadows the qualities of the religious leaders which Jesus will encounter. When Herod hears the good news, he and all of Jerusalem are troubled. What should be the cause for rejoicing is immediately felt as threat. Herod responds hypocritically. He finds out the exact time the star appeared and tells the astrologers that, if they are successful in their search, they should come back and tell him so he, too, can pay homage. Of course, he had no intentions of paying homage, and the time of the star told him at what age he would begin his slaughter. When the man Jesus will confront the religious leaders of his day, he will face a Herod-like crowd that is threatened, hypocritical, and murderous.

Luke's birth and boyhood stories also reflect themes from the life of Jesus. What happens around Jesus the baby, Jesus the man makes happen around him. Mary is the perfect disciple. She is the lowly one whom the Lord looks on and favors, and she hears God's word and keeps it. This prefigures the emphasis in Jesus' message on trusting in what God has promised and his special solidarity with the poor.

The angels sing of glory to God and peace among people. These are the twin themes of Jesus' call to repentance—praising God for God's wondrous deeds and restoring the wholeness of creation, reconciling the relationships to God, one another, the natural world, and one's own self.

The angel comes uninvited to the virgin. This symbolizes that the conception of Jesus is initiated by a free act of God. Grace and not human striving produces the person and life of Jesus. This emphasis on divine initiative will be the distinguishing feature of Jesus' preaching about the Kingdom. The priority of grace and God's unconditional love will inform his every action and be the explosive energy of his greatest parable about the prodigal father. The one who is born of grace lives from grace.

As a boy of twelve, Jesus goes to Jerusalem at Passover and is lost for three days. His parents seek him sorrowing, and when he is found, he tells them that he must be in his Father's house. At the conclusion of Jesus' career, he will to Jerusalem at Passover, die, and be lost to his disciples. He will appear to them in his risen reality and tell them he is with his Father. In the world of story, the man is in the child the way the oak is in the acorn.

These are a few of the themes foreshadowed in the infancy narratives of Matthew and Luke—the scandal of God's ways, the tension between law and love, the hypocrisy of leaders, the trust and obedience of the disciple, divine love of the poor, the radical gift of grace, and the destiny of death and resurrection. There are others—the relationship of Jesus and John, Jesus as the fulfillment of the promises of the First or Old Testament, the continuity and discontinuity of Jesus and Israel, the tension between the Jews and the Gentiles, the warning to the rich, the role of Rome, the meal ministry, and the emphasis on the heart and its treasure. What is writ small in the boy is writ large in the man.

But the process does not stop there. As we have suggested, the stories are handed down to us not only with their original meanings but with subsequent meanings that tradition has attached to them. If Matthew and Luke took mature reflections on the life, death, and resurrection of Jesus and with the help of First Testament symbolism retrojected them into infancy stories, the later Christian tradition can hardly be blamed for doing the same thing.

The process of signaling the significance of Jesus through construing his birth in a certain manner did not stop with the evangelists. Christians continued to reflect on the salvific truth of Jesus and to express that truth by focusing on the meaning of his birth. Specifically, Christians combined the theological prologue of the Gospel of John with the narratives of Matthew and Luke. Matthew and Luke became the concrete recital of how the Word became flesh. Three different prologues merged in the popular imagination to form one story, and the punch line was "The baby is God."

The truth that Christians discovered through reflection on the life of Jesus in the light of his Spirit is captured in the code word *incarnation*. Many argue that this is the central affirmation of Christian faith. It says that God's commitment to the human adventure is not a word of promise from a distant reality but a personal union with a human life. This expression of the truth about Jesus has been one of the most fruitful ideas in the history of Christianity. The doctrine of the incarnation is a revelation aimed at the person who is not sure of the worth of created existence.

God has entered the human condition. That which is most powerful—God—has become that which is most vulnerable—

a baby. Why would the divine do this? Only love does such things. Divine reality unites with human weakness out of superabundant love. Therefore, human life has been sanctified from within. There can never be any doubt about the value of created existence because God has chosen to share it with us. Also since God is one of us, we will never be abandoned. Jesus is a covenant of flesh which cannot be revoked. In the course of Christian history, these reflections developed, stabilized, and attached themselves to the birth of Jesus.

It can hardly be denied that incarnation theology combined with Matthean and Lukan narrative has proved a potent mix. It is a Christmas drink that has warmed the hardest of hearts.[6] Christmas is a time of conversion, as Dickens and all confessors know so well. But it is also a time of eye-popping wonder and mind-blowing mystery. This is the thrust of the Schillebeeckx interview which opened this chapter. His first contact with Jesus was through a Christmas crib scene with his mother singing carols and, as he later mentions, his father telling him "the baby is God."

"What were your feelings when you heard those words 'That baby is God'?" asked the interviewer. "They are difficult to describe. I experienced a feeling of awe," responded Schillebeeckx. Later he calls it an emotion of mystery.[7] A small child looks at an even smaller child and is told by one whose authority has yet to be questioned that the greatest of all realities is that baby. The impact of Christmas is meant to fascinate us beyond our capacities to understand.

No one has rung the changes on the mystery of Christmas as well as Chesterton. He knows the paradox: "that the hands that had made the sun and the stars were too small to reach the huge heads of the cattle. Upon this paradox, we might almost say upon this jest, all the literature of our faith is founded."[8] For Chesterton, it is just this joining of heaven and earth, this combining of "the idea of a baby and the idea of an unknown strength that sustains the stars" that communicates the full meaning of Jesus' life. The birth of Jesus told as the incarnation of divine love both astonishes and liberates us.

> The truth is that there is a quite peculiar and individual character about the hold of this story on human nature . . . It does not exactly in the ordinary sense turn our mind to greatness . . . It is rather something that surprises us from behind, from the hidden and personal part of our being; like that which can sometimes take us off our guard in the pathos of small objects or the blind pieties of the poor. It is rather as if a man had found an inner room in the very heart of his own house, which he had never suspected; and seen a light from within. It is as if he found something at the back of his own heart that betrayed him into good.[9]

Chesterton says this cryptically in one of his poems. "In the place where God was homeless/all men are at home."

When the truth of the incarnation merges with the infancy narratives, it combines the smallness of a baby with the greatness of God, and we are fascinated. This mightily contrasts with our normal way of thinking. In a very real way, God as a baby prepares us for the other great contrast of the gospel—God as a crucified man. Both are vulnerable figures and their intimate connection with divine reality forever changes our understanding of God, babies, and crucified people.

Also, the story of the birth of God liberates us from the deepest and darkest fear, the fear which many people think is the energy of our destructiveness. Perhaps we are not loved by the ultimate power of life. But when this final power becomes one of us and risks the dangers of human living, we know we are prized, and we are freed to live life as sons and daughters of God. This contrast and liberation cause astonishment, and we praise God.

But are we drawn to the man whose life provoked this great truth? Does the incarnational interpretation of the infancy narratives breed desire? When we are carried away by the religious experience of Christmas, are we carried toward the man the child will grow up to be?

The truth of the incarnation was generated by reflection on the life, death, and resurrection of Jesus in the light of the divine promises made to Israel. It is perhaps the premier expression of the event of God reconciling the world in Christ (2 Cor. 5:19). It was attached to the birth of Jesus as an enticement to ponder the life of Jesus. If it becomes an isolated metaphysical assertion about the origins of Jesus, it loses its potential as a lure.

The birth of Jesus must stay connected to the whole story and not disengage itself and become a lonely but glorious truth. This is the perspective that our brief literary analysis of the Gospels provided. The birth narratives are wondrous foreshadowings which are meant to lure us to the life of the man who was born with such fanfare. Who will this God-Man grow up to be and what will he do?

Risen From The Dead

The resurrection of Jesus is confessed but not narrated. We are told in one of the early Church's first creeds that he was raised from the dead on the third day according to the Scriptures (1 Cor. 15:3–7). And Peter forthrightly proclaims:

> God freed him [Jesus] from death's bitter pangs, however, and raised him up again, for it was impossible that death should keep its hold on him

> . . . This is the Jesus God has raised up, and we are his witnesses.
>
> Acts 2:24, 32

But they were not witnesses to the act of resurrection itself. Ezekiel in his famous vision may see bones rattle and join to other bones and "sinew and the flesh come upon them" (Ez. 37:7–8). But nothing like that is said about Jesus. We have stories about an empty tomb, but we have no eyewitness accounts of Jesus' coming back to life.

We have empty tomb plus message stories and appearance narratives. These twin sets of stories can be approached in the same way as the infancy narratives. We can try to hear the stories as intriguing tales. Then we can consider the pastoral, apologetic, and theological concerns they originally reflected. Finally, we will take note of the dominant theological interpretation which has been attached to them. Out of this mix what fascinates us about the risen Christ may be more fully specified.

The details of the empty tomb stories differ from gospel to gospel, but the impact of the empty tomb (empty of Jesus' body but filled with messengers) on the people is remarkably similar. In Matthew, the women hurry away from the empty tomb and the angel's message "half-overjoyed, half-fearful" (Mt. 28:8).

Mark's famous last line has the women fleeing the tomb bewildered and trembling, unable to take the white-robed young man's advice "You need not be amazed!" (Mk. 16:6). When the women in Luke tell the disciples the tomb is empty, Peter goes to investigate and finds nothing but the wrappings. "So he went away full of amazement at what had occurred" (Lk. 24:12).

In John, Magdalene thinks the body has been stolen; Peter stares at the linen wrappings, seemingly without comprehension; the beloved disciple looks at the emptiness of the tomb and believes (Jn. 20:1–10). These people are confused; fearful; amazed; and, at best, half-believing. What is causing this flurry of responses is something they did not expect and something they cannot fathom.

No matter how historians reconstruct the relationship between the empty tomb and the appearance narratives, in the Gospels the connection is quite clear. The empty tomb stories tell us Jesus is not in the grave; the appearance stories tell us where he is. He is doing what he did during his life, gathering his dispersed disciples, healing and commissioning them. Many had abandoned him during his arrest, trial, and execution. Some of the disciples, mostly women, followed him to the end and saw it all. But in a real sense, everyone was crucified with Christ. His death engulfed them all. When he rose, he came back to make sure they all rose with him.

Hunted men in a locked room see what they missed—the wounds of Jesus. They are told to be peaceful and to go forth out of the locked room (Jn. 20:19–23). A doubting man wants to probe the wounds and is given the chance. He does not take it but believes anyway (Jn. 20:24–29). A guilty man in a boat recognizes the Lord on the shore, knows he is as naked as Adam, puts on clothes, and jumps in the water. Later he will be asked three times by the Lord, "Do you love me?" He will say "yes" each time, but the third time there will be no boast in his voice (Jn. 21:1–17). A woman of grief cannot be consoled until she hears her name from the one she cannot find (Jn. 20:11–18). Two youths are disillusioned and do not understand until the Scriptures are opened and the bread broken (Lk. 24:13–35). Disciples who are "incredulous for sheer joy" laugh their way to belief when Jesus asks them for something to eat (Lk. 24:36–49). And all are commissioned.

These are stories of reunion and commissioning. As stories, they tap into the high emotions of all "separation-reunion" tales. But in these stories, the stakes are higher for two reasons. What separates the people is death and they are all in need of healing from the one who is to return. His return means their conversion—from fear to peace, from doubt to faith, from guilt to forgiveness, from grief to joy, from disillusionment to hope. All the resurrection stories are about the concomitant coming back to life of Jesus and his friends.

Caryll Houselander has explored the resurrection stories as exquisite portrayals of Jesus' sensitivity to people.[10] To the prostitute Magdalene, he spoke the tenderness of her name, asked of her spiritual love, and commissioned her as an apostle. To the fearful men of the upper room, he spoke the word their hearts hoped for—"peace." He taught both the intellectuals on the road to Emmaus and the plain and simple Thomas the truth about wounds, but in a way both could understand. And he coaxed from Peter a threefold love that would assuage his threefold guilt. By modern standards, Houselander's interpretation of the stories is fanciful. But she does focus on these tales as intriguing human stories and not merely narrative examples of pastoral and theological concerns.

These twin sets of resurrection stories—empty tomb and appearances—reflect many of the concerns of the early Church. Some of these are the ambiguity of the experience of the risen Lord and the difficulty in recognizing him; the physicality of the risen body; the connection between the risen Lord and the crucified Jesus; the relationship between those who had experienced the risen Lord and those who had not; the nature of faith in the risen Lord; the relationship between resurrection, ascension, and sending of the Spirit; the ambiguity of the empty tomb evidence; and the effect of the experience of the risen Christ on those who encountered him. All these stories carry some kind of response to one or more of these concerns.

The major theological motif popularly associated with the resurrection is simple yet startling—risen from the dead. Although the stories deal primarily with Jesus' relationship with his followers, the doctrine of the resurrection deals primarily with Jesus' relationship to God. Divine reality sustained Jesus through the terrors of death and brought him into a transformed existence.

This transformed existence is not only explored in the empty tomb and appearance narratives, but it is further developed through the symbols of ascension and exaltation. Jesus is with the Father in heaven as the co-sender of the Spirit. Therefore, his resurrection indicates a dual presence. His resurrected body is "at the right hand of the Father," and his Spirit animates his followers and forms them into his new earthly body. He is permanently present, but in different ways: both with God in heaven and among the company of his followers on earth.

But in subsequent reflection, this destiny of Jesus with God was taken for granted. What was highlighted was the victory over death. Despite its horror, death does not have the last word. Physical death has given way to new life. But it is not just physical death that has been vanquished. All the death-dealing forces which haunt human life have been given notice.

The powers that crush us—guilt, fear, self-hatred, alienation, grief—will not ultimately claim us. Did not Jesus come back to free his friends from their entrapment by these forces? The brief "story patterns" from H. A. Williams which opened this chapter are examples of the power of the resurrection in the present. The resurrection of Jesus means that the power of

God has relativized the forces of destruction, and the pattern of death and resurrection is the pattern of participation in divine reality.

This theological appropriation of the resurrection stories fascinates us because it liberates us from fear and astonishes us at a level we can barely believe. The human heart is continually concerned with the status of what it cherishes in the face of the destructiveness of life. It is fearful that what it prizes will be swept away.

We know our love does not match our power. If we could, we would, but we cannot. When we hear that divine love and power suffuses and supplements our own, our fear of loss subsides. We are capable of changing the panicky and self-defeating ways in which we live and relate. This possibility makes us, as Luke's story suggests, "incredulous for sheer joy." The risen reality of Christ communicates a joy we cannot believe. We cannot believe it because it is the fulfillment of our deepest desires. Quite simply, it is too good to be true.

When the resurrection stories are interpreted through this theological lens, we see ourselves and our world in a new way. But we can also be shortsighted. The incarnation interpretation of the infancy narratives had a tendency to become a glorious but isolated truth. Only by returning to the original dynamics of the narrative were we forced forward to consider the life of Jesus. The "overcoming of death" interpretation of the resurrection stories can also become a glorious but isolated truth. But if we return to some of the original concerns of those stories, we will be forced back to the life of Jesus.

It is not just anyone who is raised from the dead. It is Jesus of Nazareth who was handed over by the religious authorities and executed by the State, and the stories are at pains to make that clear. The risen Lord speaks and acts in ways that show he is the pre-Easter Jesus. He displays the wounds of crucifixion; he eats with his apostles; he recommissions them; and he interprets the meaning of his own life. One of the primitive understandings of the resurrection is that it vindicates the life and message of Jesus. His death cast into doubt his mission; his resurrection means divine approval. The resurrection forces the question "Who was this man whom God raised from the dead?"

Both Christmas and Easter fascinate us because they contrast with the way we normally think, answer a pressing question of the human heart, and astonish us. Where they have been traditionally weak is in creating the desire to apprentice ourselves to the One who was born in such a way and was raised in such a way. One reason for this is that the astonishing theology of birth and resurrection obscured the "leanings" of the primary narratives. But birth and resurrection drive us to the life and death of Jesus. It is this life which we must now explore.

CHAPTER THREE

Fascination with Jesus: Life and Death

I believe that there is nothing on earth more beautiful, more profound, more virile, or more perfect than Christ; and I say to myself, with jealous love, that greater than he does not and cannot exist. More than this: should anyone prove to me that Christ is beyond the range of truth, and that all this is not to be found in him, I would prefer to retain Christ than to retain the truth.[1]

Feodor Dostoyevski

Ah! there was a heart right!
There was single eye![2]

Gerard Manley Hopkins

We have explored the power of the birth and resurrection stories to fascinate us. They touch our heart in its twin vulnerabilities—the fear we are not loved and the suspicion that destruction is the final word. Christmas and Easter carry the good news of the baby who is God and the man risen from the dead. But when we closely examined the birth and resurrection stories in their original settings, we saw that they do not stand on their own. They are the wonderful beginning and extraordinary ending to a whirlwind middle. It is this middle, the life and death of Jesus, which has more "native" power to claim us and create that facet of fascination we have called desire.

We will approach the life and death of Jesus by examining the Gospels from both a historical and a literary point of view. We are not interested in these two methods in themselves, and so we will not engage in arguments about their relative merits. Both these methods are complementary and are interwoven in any concrete act of interpretation. Our exploration hopes to uncover a Jesus who seriously draws us into a decision about whether to apprentice ourselves to him. In my opinion, both historical and literary approaches uncover an original and startling person. He is one who knows how to live and die and, therefore, has the power to make a genuine claim on us who must also live and die.

In both the historical and literary portraits which we will etch, we will return to our approach of Chapter One. We will concentrate, although not exclusively, on the horizontal dimension of Jesus' life. We will note the outlooks, attitudes, and actions of Jesus as he interacts with his contemporaries. If we find some response which attracts us, we may ask how we can make it our own. If we find a series of responses which leap out to make a claim on us and offer us a way of life which we have been secretly looking for, then we may begin the process of apprenticeship. Avery Dulles admits he cannot completely explain it but tries to describe this response to Jesus:

What is it about Jesus Christ that impels me, as it has impelled millions of others, to address him in divine terms and to turn to him in an attitude of prayer and worship? I suspect that none of us can really explain. All I can say is that, like many others, I have experienced in contemplating Jesus a shock of recognition: it is as though he were the very person I had been looking for and had not been able to find.[3]

If this occurs, then we will want Jesus to introduce us to the power that inspires and sustains his creative way of living and dying. This is the vertical dimension of his life—his relationship to God, whom he calls "Abba!" In order to contact and communicate with this reality, we will have to undergo the rigors of discipleship.

A Historical Portrait

The historical approach to the life and death of Jesus takes seriously the fact that the Gospels are products of a complex historical development. In Catholic theology, it is commonplace to distinguish and interrelate three levels—the words and deeds of Jesus, the apostolic preaching, and the final authorship of the evangelist. In order to clarify these levels, the wholistic Gospels must be disassembled and reassembled. In response to the question "What was your aim in the Jesus book?" Schillebeeckx clearly laid out the path of this project.

> My main intention was to disassociate the story of Jesus from all that dogmatic theology and to go back to that man, Jesus of Nazareth, who appeared in that place and at that time. And then to follow the whole of that way—what he said and did and how his apostles reacted to what he said and did and above all how they reacted to his death on the cross.[4]

If this reconstruction is undertaken effectively, we can trace the development from the words and deeds of Jesus to the final gospel portraits. Our reward will be an in-depth understanding of the faith development of the early Church and, to the degree we are capable of making the translation, perspectives and guidelines for Christian faith today.

There is more than a little hesitation about this enterprise. One concern is the historical-critical method itself. This approach varies with what is currently considered reliable historiography and with the convincing and skillful execution of the historian's craft. In the not-so-distant past, it was judged that the Gospels contained very little historical material. The early Christian communities had so transformed the oral and written Jesus traditions that very little of "reliable memory" remained.

Today, the judgment is more generous. The historical material in the Gospels is, if not abundant, considerable. We can reconstruct the words and deeds of Jesus with a decent degree of probability. But whatever the current "state of the art" is, it must be remembered that what is under fire is not primarily the Gospels but the historical tools we have constructed.

But for Catholic sensibility, the more "nervous estimation" of the quest for the historical Jesus concerns the possible outcome. The bias of Catholic theology is that there has been a legitimate development between scriptural christological affirmations and later dogmatic statements. Although there may be differences, there has not been a break. The discontinuities in the tradition are part of a larger continuity.

Now this same question of "break" has been extended into the Gospels themselves. What if the Gospels are taken apart and they cannot be put back together again? We may find ourselves unwittingly acting out the Humpty Dumpty nursery rhyme. We push the four wholistic portraits of Jesus Christ off the wall, and perhaps all the king's horses and all the king's men cannot put him back together again.

In other words, there is a lot riding on this reassembling effort. If there is no continuity between Jesus' life and message, how his disciples interpreted him, and how the evangelist portrayed him, our faith takes its origin from Paul or Peter and not from Jesus. This fear is what George Bernard Shaw called the "monstrous imposition on Jesus." He stressed the extreme discontinuity between the man Jesus and the movement that used his name:

It was Paul who converted the religion that has raised one man above sin and death into a religion that delivered millions of men so completely into their domination that their own common nature became a horror to them, and the religious life became a denial of life.[5]

Although very few would accept this judgment today, this is the type of perspective which can emerge when the historical-critical method is used in an exclusively antagonistic fashion. It also occasioned the quiver of doubt in Dostoyevski's beautiful tribute to Christ which opened this chapter. If someone would tell Dostoevski that Christ is not the truth, he would prefer to retain Christ and jettison the truth. There is no need for this extreme gesture.

With these hesitations in mind, what is the benefit of this approach? From our point of view, it is an attempt to trace the original path of fascination. It wants to uncover the words of Jesus in that momentous silence between the time they were spoken and the time people spoke back. It wants to find the "split second" between the actions of Jesus and the reactions of people who knelt, spat, shouted, threw rocks, and ripped garments.

This is an effort to reconstruct the original contrasts, liberations, astonishments, desires, and envies which surrounded the person of Jesus. To the extent that this can be done and to the extent we have the energy to engage in this laborious process, we may reclaim the gospel tradition from within. If we do, we may encounter anew the claim of Jesus which creates the desire for discipleship.

The portrait of the historical Jesus begins by using sophisticated diagnostic tools to gather historically reliable material.[6] Although the assessment of what is historically reliable fluctuates, there are some constant candidates.

Jesus came from Nazareth in Galilee.

He was baptized by John the Baptist, and in all likelihood, it was a momentous event in his life.

He preached the nearness of the Kingdom of God and connected its advent with his words and deeds.

He was a teacher who used stories and images to express and communicate his vision.

He was a prophet who criticized the existing state of Israelite religion and called people to a new vision of God, Israel, and the individual.

He was an exorcist and healer and interpreted these deeds as signs of God's power.

He gathered disciples around himself and commissioned them to continue his mission.

He was in continual conflict with the religious authority on a series of issues centering on the relationship between law, sin, and righteousness.

He attacked the Temple cult and its priestly administrators.

He called God "Abba" and claimed, at least implicitly, unique relationship with him.

He gathered people who were considered outcasts and sinners together and ate and drank with them.

He was betrayed by one of his followers and denied by many more.

He was crucified as a political pretender by the Roman authorities and considered a blasphemer by the Jewish authorities.

This list of facts could be expanded, but it is enough raw data to trigger the next move. Few people let facts lie there. They try to relate these perceptions to one another to tell a consistent and credible story. What is the hidden unity which will hold this collection of accurate appraisals in dynamic tension? What picture of Jesus can be painted with the colors that historical inquiry has provided? There has been no dearth of painters and each portrait looks slightly different.

Elizabeth Johnson has suggested these summaries for some of the major contemporary attempts:

The eschatological prophet announcing God's nearness in the midst of suffering and embodying the joy of this in his liberating life-style (Schillebeeckx); the critical reformer proclaiming God's will for human well-being in the face of institution, hierarchy and law (Kung); the Spirit-filled man of faith and obedience mediating the Spirit of freedom to others (Kasper); the opposer of injustice in the name of God whose call to discipleship involves the faithful follower in the same suffering fate (Sobrino).[7]

When these capsule assessments are thoroughly explored, we may encounter a man who knows how to live and die and whom we may want to follow.

Identity

We will explore only three aspects of a historical portrait and suggest interpretations which may intrigue us. The first focuses on Jesus' self-understanding. It is difficult to determine if Jesus used titles about himself or, if he did, which ones he used and how he understood them. According to different scholars, he may have referred to himself as the Son or the Son of Man or the Suffering Servant or the Prophet of the Last Days.[8] But perhaps Joseph Fitzmyer states the most common appraisal:

With the possible exception of "Son of Man," there is no evidence that the earthly Jesus ever used these titles of himself.[9]

Part of the enigma of Jesus is his refusal to use titles to identify himself.

But where Jesus was reticent, others were ready. During his lifetime, people certainly addressed him with titles, and after his death, the early Church marshaled both Jewish and Hellenistic titles to try to explore the mystery of his life and person. But no matter who used the titles—Jesus' contemporaries, the early Church, or even Jesus himself—the titles themselves were transformed once they made contact with Jesus. Who Jesus was could not be captured in one title or in an accumulation of titles. His reality shattered categories imposed on him. If the tendency in the general course of culture is for titles to swallow the person, in the case of Jesus the reverse occurred. The person of Jesus absorbed every title applied to him, changed its meaning, and transcended it.

This fact—that cultural categories cannot hold Jesus—leads us to examine a more subtle set of claims. There is an implicit self-understanding in Jesus' whole style of relating. What is the underlying self-understanding of a man who calls God "Abba" and begins sentences with "Amen," signifying divine approval of what he is about to say before he has even said it? What prompts a man to respond with a story about how God acts when he is challenged about the way he acts? What is behind the claim that he uses the finger of God to cast out devils when everyone knows the finger of God wrote the law on Sinai? What is implied when a man uses his own experience and "intuitive sense of God's will" to challenge the Mosaic law? Where does the nerve come from to suggest that if we do not respond to him, we are not responding to God? In other words, much of what we know about Jesus suggests that he understood himself to be in a unique relationship to God and to have a unique role in salvation history.

There is something fascinating about a man whose importance is so secure he has no need of establishing it by arrogating titles to himself. Titles force people into prescribable behavior. What is protocol when faced with the Son of Man? Deference replaces genuine response. So he never pointed to himself and said, "Kneel!"

But Jesus did interrupt people's lives with a presence so graceful yet demanding that they associated it with God, and except when he sensed it to be insincere, he allowed that association to stand. His importance was in what he was making happen. Authority is known because new life is being "authored," not because titles are being claimed. His identity was always there, but it was never brought out as a club to make people submit. Jesus' unique relationship to God was the implicit claim that was never claimed.

Yet it was a claim and not a modest one. It may have been implicit, but it was real, and we have suggested that the titles were shunned or shattered because the claim was too much for them. To put it mildly, this claim to uniqueness contrasts with what we expect. Chesterton pointed this out years ago, and if we purify his argument with more refined exegesis, we may share his perception of a "most curious and interesting" problem.[10]

It seems that the greater a man is, the less he claims. This is especially true about his relationship to God. The great saints are the first to confess their sinfulness. "The only kind of man that ever makes that kind of claim (the very greatest) is a very small man."[11] Yet Jesus makes a great claim and is obviously not a small man. With this start, Chesterton moves us along his apologetic path.

Divinity is great enough to be divine; it is great enough to call itself divine. But as humanity grows greater, it grows less and less likely to do so. God is God, as the Moslems say; but a great man knows he is not God, and the greater he is the better he knows it. That is the paradox; everything that is merely approaching to that point is merely receding from it. Socrates, the wisest man, knows that he knows nothing. A lunatic may think he is omniscience, and a fool may talk as if he were omniscient. But Christ is in another sense omniscient if he not only knows, but knows that he knows.[12]

Chesterton's presuppositions have been substantially challenged by modern theology. We do not have direct access to Jesus' inner world and bold contrasts between the divine and human in Jesus do not seem to honor the complexity of the hypostatic union. But his overall point is still "intensely interesting."[13] In Jesus' words and actions, there is a claim to a relationship to God which great men and women, precisely because they are close to God, would find close to blasphemous.

Jesus of Nazareth is a man who exudes power and importance but refuses to claim the cultural titles of importance. He relies on what he does to convey who he is. Yet the implicit claim of his words and actions is monumental, the type of claim vain, petty, and insecure men and women make. Yet if ever there was a person who was not vain, petty, or insecure, it was Jesus. But we might object that he was not so special to God. He died a horrible death at the hands of people who hated him. If he was God's Son, he would have been spared that. Here the mystery deepens, for it was because he was God's Son that he died on the cross.

Death

A second aspect of the portrait of the historical Jesus which is fascinating concerns his attitude toward his death. The early Church was squarely faced with the scandal of Jesus' death. The One whom they were proclaiming as the Risen Lord was crucified as a criminal. His ignominious death had to be explained and a number of explanations developed. The immediate choice was a simple contrast. Sin had killed Jesus: God had raised him. But in this interpretation the death of Jesus had no positive value. It was merely a manifestation of the power of sin which the power of God overcame. So other interpretations were developed which stressed the death as part of a divine plan and as an atoning sacrifice.

This movement to a more positive evaluation of the death of Jesus may have had its inspiration in Jesus' own attitude. Jesus did not need supernatural knowledge to see that his death was imminent. The execution of his forerunner, John the Baptist, and the growing hostility of the religious leaders were clear signs that his mission would not be accepted and that he would share the fate of a prophet. But it seems that Jesus' sense of divine purpose was so strong that he integrated his rejection into the divine plan.

On the basis of critically justified exegesis, it is essential to affirm Jesus' integration of his violent death into his surrender of himself to God and his offer of salvation to men. Despite this, however, it is impossible to deny the negativity of that death, as a rejection.[14]

Jesus saw his death as a loving service to people and a "handing over of himself" to his Father.

The logic of Jesus' handing himself over to his Father can be readily understood. Throughout his life Jesus trusted in God. He received his life from God and gave his life back to God. Death for Jesus was the peak and culminating moment of that process. Death can be a time when we sum up life, when we, in our radical freedom, dispose of ourselves in a total way. Either we abandon ourselves to the mystery from which we came and to which we return or we curse our life and fate. Jesus' death is an act of trust in God. He offers his spirit to the God who sent the Spirit upon him. The dynamic is life from God, life in God, life to God.

But Jesus's death is not only an event of trust between himself and his Father. It is also a salvific event between himself and people, especially between himself and his executioners. This is not so easily understood. It is one thing to say that Jesus held onto his convictions to the end and demanded that people repent and change their lives. This would be understandable, and certainly it was part of a true prophet's expected behavior. But it is difficult to interpret this type of adamancy as loving service. We have to move to a deeper, more personal level to grasp the death of Jesus as a mix of love and service.

The double commandment of love, toward God and toward neighbor, motivated Jesus' life. This love energy suffused an other-centered life of service. But this service was not the service of servility. It was sustained attention to the liberation of people from whatever forces oppressed them.

One set of powerful oppressive forces which people seldom reflect on is the violence of society which they have internalized. Our own violence is the sin closest to home. It was precisely this violence, unleashed and at full fury, that was directed at Jesus. To resist it would be to multiply it. To receive it into his own person as an act of love would be to bear it away. The violent may bear the Kingdom away, but the loving bear violence away. "He took away the sin of the world" is an experiential truth before it is a theological conviction. Or, as van Beeck puts it, "Loving one's enemy is suffering for him at his own hands."[15] This is a type of service only the servant of God understands.

Christians have always connected the death of Jesus with the salvation of the world. But it is fascinating to note that from one perspective Jesus' death was "salvific" for himself. Most of us, in our imagination, envision even a "happy death" as a brutal interruption of our plans. It is the end of life and we resent it, but bolstered by the cynical wisdom that "no one gets out alive," we are resigned.

But if our lot is an "unhappy death," a death too soon or in agony or in humiliation, it is a horror which casts a shadow over whatever our lives may have accomplished. But Jesus, victimized into an "unhappy death," transforms it from a contradiction of his life into its culminating act. This is not life cut short; it is, as the Johannine redactor so clearly saw, life accomplished:

> When Jesus took the wine, he said, "Now it is finished." Then he bowed his head, and delivered over his spirit.
>
> John 19:30

Inclusiveness

A third aspect of the historical portrait of Jesus concerns the dynamics of inclusiveness and exclusiveness. Jesus interacts with all levels of Hebrew society, from religious elite to social outcast. No one seems automatically excluded from his concern or company. Jesus' inclusiveness is usually described in terms of the "ins and outs" of society. Those whom the societal leaders spurned, Jesus embraced. Jesus ate and drank with "tax collectors and sinners," an umbrella category for the religiously unclean and the socially unacceptable. The leaders saw this table fellowship as blurring the boundaries between the righteous and the sinner and questioning the whole idea of purity within Judaism. We know that when Jesus ate and drank with "tax collectors" and sinners, he alienated the religious leaders. What we do not know is if when Jesus ate and drank with the religious leaders, he alienated the tax collectors and sinners.

Jesus also reached out to the poor. He counted himself among them because he had "nowhere to lay his head" (Lk. 9:58). He preached to them that they had a dignity which no societal estimation could compromise. The opening line of the beatitudes is as startling today as in Jesus' time: "Blest are you poor" (Lk. 6:20). He excoriated the leaders because they tinkered with religious trivia and were numb to the plight of the poor. "You pay tithes on mint and herbs and seeds while neglecting the weightier matters of the law, justice and mercy and good faith" (Mt. 23:23). As it is often remarked, Jesus afflicted the comfortable and comforted the afflicted.

Another group severely constricted by society were women. Jesus' relationship with women broke many of the customs and conventions of his day. He talked to women in public; he allowed a prostitute to undo her hair and anoint his feet; he had close women friends and some of his disciples were women. The overall picture is that whatever society had dismissed, disvalued, or forgotten, Jesus pursued. A remark whose basic intentionality may go back to Jesus says it simply: "The Son of Man has come to search out and save what was lost" (Lk. 19:10).

The depth of this inclusive spirit of Jesus was only fully realized when the Jewish Christian community faced the question of the admission of Gentiles. Is Jesus just for us or for all people? Or put in more generic terms, should any group as a group be excluded? The New Testament gives ample evidence that this was one of the most vexing questions for the followers of Jesus, and the inspiration for what many consider the boldest story of the Gospels.

A Canaanite woman begs Jesus for a cure for her daughter (Mt. 15:21–28; Mk. 7:25–30). He refuses on the grounds that she is not a Jew. She cleverly persists, taking Jesus' insulting image that "it is not right to take the food of the children and throw it to the dogs" and turning it back on him: "even the dogs under the table eat the family's leavings." Her persistent faith persuades Jesus to change his mind. Her daughter is cured. Peter's remark might provide the appropriate gloss: "I begin to see how true it is that God shows no partiality" (Acts 10:34).

It seems that Jesus restricted his activity to the people of Israel. But within Israel he was open to all the diverse factions. The followers of Jesus only gradually saw that this spirit of openness extended to all people. Although Jesus was a Jew, there was something universal in his approach and outlook. He did not exclude anybody on the basis of group affiliation or on the unchosen givens of the human condition. The automatic dichotomies of human life were not honored. The Epistle to the Galatians captures it: "There does not exist among you Jew or Greek, slave or freeman, male or female. All are one in Christ Jesus" (3:28).

There are two major dangers associated with an inclusive community. The first is homogenization. Everyone is reduced to the least common denominator. Distinctiveness is lost in the name of uniformity. This does not seem to be the case in Jesus' understanding and practice of inclusivity. John Haught calls Jesus' way the "harmonizing of contrasts":

In the story of Jesus the Christian is attracted to the expansiveness of the man from Nazareth who reaches out in the broadest possible way in order to integrate into his life the widest variety of people and experiences. The integration and harmonizing of contrasts is what gives his life a beauty that is compelling and healing to the believer, and that leads the Christian to understand him as the embodiment of ultimate beauty, as somehow divine. The story pictures Jesus as embracing tax collectors, prostitutes, rich and poor, the socially respected and the socially rejected, women as well as men, children and adults, heretics along with the orthodox, the sick and the healthy. He is pictured as himself a story teller in whose stories there is equally vivid harmonizing of contrasts: a father embracing a prodigal son, a tax collector praying for forgiveness; a heretic showing a compassion far surpassing that of the orthodox, an employer rewarding laggards with the same wages as those who have worked a full day. Jesus' imagination is full of such jarring juxtapositions. And, the story goes, Jesus' own existence synthesizes the apparent contradictions of a healthy love for life with an attitude of openness to execution. It is the harmony of such sharp contrasts that summons forth our appreciation of this man.[16]

Jesus does not level people to make them one. He heightens their distinctiveness to make them a communion of unique persons.

The second danger is "repressive tolerance." Everyone does his or her own thing and goes his or her own way, and it is "all OK." All attitudes and behaviors are tolerated to such an extent that the tolerance itself becomes repressive. This was hardly the case with Jesus. All the evidence points to him as a very divisive character. His inclusive stance does not lead to a repressively tolerant community but to a new basis for discerning the "ins and the outs." When people do not respond to Jesus' invitation, they exclude themselves.

The parable of the great banquet suggests that God through Jesus is planning a feast. But those invited have other things to do. The consequence of this is that they will be excluded. They received an invitation, but they tore it up. Jesus is a universal offer who meets with persistent and particular refusals. The paradox is that the invitation to an inclusive community generates its own form of exclusion.

It is important to note that the inclusion-exclusion dynamics which Jesus precipitates occur on the level of person. James Breech has made a strong case that Jesus' parables all emphasize people in the midst of action.[17] For the most part, the group affiliation of these people is not mentioned, or if it is, it is often because they are about to engage in actions which will contradict the stereotype of that group (e.g. the good Samaritan). In other words, Jesus' imagination, as reflected in his stories, is drawn to those life situations where unique persons, unable to be reduced to their sex, race, or religion, are acting and reacting. This is the arena of the human, where the Kingdom of God is active and where Jesus meets people.

This facet of Jesus can be easily turned into a platitude. We glibly assert that we are not prejudiced, that we take each person on his or her merits. But on close examination, prejudice is the constant companion of the human condition. Groups maintain boundaries and identities through processes of automatic discrimination. What we try not to be is unfashionably prejudiced. Discrimination against people of color is "out," but a bureaucrat is a bureaucrat down to the bottom button of his vest.

The truth seems to be that we move through a series of prejudices which our group fosters for its own sense of worth and survival. This blindness is so thorough that we often do not recognize it and proudly profess our openness to all. What is fascinating and liberating about Jesus is that he encountered the next person met as precisely that, the next person met. Of course they belonged to social groups and religious and political philosophies, but they were not mere instances of larger, abstract categories.

We have dipped the brush of imagination into the colors of historical facts, and painted a few of the features of Jesus. He is a man whose words and deeds imply a heightened sense of importance and identity. But it is an identity he is reluctant to reveal. He would rather allow his words and deeds to speak for him than to claim an exalted title and demand people respond because of who he is. He faced his death squarely and turned this greatest moment of weakness into a manifestation of strength. He dies at the hands of people who consider him an enemy. Yet he lovingly receives their violence and so frees them, if they respond, from their terrible slavery to destruction.

The same reluctance he has to identifying himself by title and role he displays when meeting people. They are more than their place in society. She is not a prostitute but Mary. He not a fisherman but Peter, not a Pharisee but Simon, not a tax collector but Levi. Yet in each unique person is a common freedom to follow along or to walk away. The paradox is that the uniqueness of each person is the bond of our common humanity. And the proper name for the man who revealed this truth and lived in fidelity to its rigorous demands is not Messiah or King of the Jews—both titles used by those who jeer at him as he hangs on the cross—but the name the criminal who turned to him in hope used: Jesus (Lk. 23:32–42).

A Literary Portrait

As we mentioned, there can be no strict separation of historical and literary approaches to the Gospels. Historical retrieval has to begin with literary discernment, and literary methods eventually consult historical knowledge. One of the most insightful combinations of historical and literary approaches is to interrelate the historical situation of the evangelist and the gospel he produced. Internal clues in the story reflect conflicts in his community, and conflicts in his community find expression in the story. This procedure would uncover the theological portrait of the Matthean, Marcan, Lukan, Johannine Christ. But given our chosen preoccupation with fascination, there are two limitations which keep us from exploring the riches of this approach.

First, the theological portrait which emerges is stated in the images and categories of the first century. For the people of that time, these were the perfect and powerful expressions of the truth and meaning of Jesus. But for us, Jesus as the creator of a new covenant or the suffering servant of a new age or the incarnate Word does not have immediate resonance. Therefore, extensive translation would be required.[3] But it does not provide that "sudden noticing" which triggers fascination.

Second, theology is a second-order activity, reflecting and organizing more primary material. The images and categories are summary statements derived from longer and messier narratives. If we attend to this longer and messier narrative, to the actual words and actions of Jesus, we may create summary images and categories more immediately available to contemporary sensibilities. Then we might be able to merge them with the "native" images and categories of the Gospels. Along the way, a desire for discipleship may be nurtured.

Inner Dynamism

We will enrich our historical portrait of Jesus by selecting three characteristics from the gospel narratives. First, Jesus is a person of inner dynamism. He comes at life with energy and purpose. This "active quality" means that he influences the course of events more than the course of events influences him. This dynamism shows itself in his consciousness of mission and in the way he leans into situations, shaping them according to his perspectives and values.

It is often suggested that Jesus is an itinerant charismatic. He wanders through Israel, preaching to whoever is available and encountering folks on roads and in villages. Yet the portrait of Jesus is not that he wanders but that he journeys. He is a man on the move but it is not wanderlust that drives him. After he cures Peter's mother-in-law and any others, he sleeps, rises early, and goes to the desert to pray (Mk. 1:32–39). Peter finds him. "Everybody is looking for you!" But Jesus will have none of it: "Let us move on to the neighboring villages so that I may proclaim the good news there also. That is what I have come to do." Jesus is man with a mission on his mind, and although his geographical moves may not be in a straight line, they are all part of a straight purpose.

In the Gospels, everyone, at one time or another, seems perplexed about Jesus except Jesus himself. After he performs wonders, people inquire about his identity (Mk. 4:41). In a famous sequence, Jesus asks his disciples about who people think he is and then who they think he is (Mt. 16:13–20; Mk. 8:27; Lk 9:18). At his trial, his interrogators ask him directly about who he is, hoping he will say the words that will permit them to condemn him (Lk. 23:6; Mk. 14:61) .

But Jesus never seems to be in doubt about his identity and mission. This does not mean he knows all his mission will entail or that he is not faced with real decisions at every turn along the conflict-ridden road he has taken. But he is not a man searching for himself; he is a man who knows himself and is searching for others. This unequivocal firmness in the portrait of Jesus accounts for the power he brings to each encounter.

Jesus moves out of an inner energy and fullness. Perhaps it is too strong to say that he attacks life, but he is extremely assertive. His assertiveness is part of every story, but it is especially evident in the call narratives. In Mark and Matthew, Jesus watches Simon and Andrew cast their nets into the sea. He must have liked what he saw, for he immediately says, "Come after me; I will make you fishers of men" (Mk. 1:17).

In Luke, Jesus climbs uninvited into Simon's boat and asks him to pull out a short distance from the shore so that he can teach the crowds. When he is done, he orders Simon to once again go fishing, only this time with him. Simon protests but gives in to the forcefulness of the person who is asking.

In John, two disciples hear the Baptist call Jesus the lamb of God. They follow him but characteristically Jesus turns on them: "What do you want?" They said, "Where do you live?" Jesus replied, "Come and see."

At the center of each of these stories is a man capable of saying, "It was not you who chose me, it was I who chose you" (Jn. 15:16). We always read contemporary values into Jesus, but it would be difficult to find a story that would justify calling him laid-back.

Jesus finds himself in many different situations which he must quickly evaluate and respond to. Yet his responses never seem to be mere reaction. Circumstances (the disciples not understanding, the crowd-blocking petitioners, hungry people with nowhere to go, and so on) may be pushing events in a certain direction, or people sent to trap and test Jesus may be manipulating the situation for their own ends. But once Jesus intervenes, the situation is reshaped according to his will.

This does not mean that Jesus rigidly follows his own course and avoids the people who are present and the issues that are at stake. Jesus is flexible in the sense that he attends carefully to situations and people and relates in terms of the realities he perceives. But he is not flexible in the sense that he allows situations and people to dictate to him the terms of his involvement. In other words, he is not one more factor in a situation; he is the touchstone for its truth or error, for its success or failure. Everything and every person, as Simeon predicted, rises and falls in relation to him (Lk. 2:34).

The stories about people "coming at" Jesus often end with Jesus "coming at" them. Tables turn with remarkable regularity; would-be challengers find themselves challenged. A man who wants Jesus to tell his brother to give him his share of the inheritance is told instead a story about the untimely death of a barn builder (Lk. 12:13–21). A lawyer who wants to know who is his neighbor is told instead a story about how to be a neighbor (Lk. 10:25–37). A king who wants to see a miracle of action is treated instead to a miracle of silence (Lk. 23:8–9). Two disciples who want to sit at the right and the left of glory are offered instead a cup of suffering and a bath of pain (Mk. 10:35–38). Some Sadducees who want to know what seven husbands are going to do with one wife in the marriage bed of the afterlife are referred to angels (Lk.20:27–40). Some spies "in the guise of honest men" who want to know if they must pay tax to the emperor are asked instead to produce a coin (Lk. 20:20–26). This ability of Jesus to reverse challenge is a part of his active rather than reactive style. Also it makes one remark of the Gospels seem very sensible: "And no one had the courage to ask him any more questions" (Mk. 12:34).

The situation where Jesus would seem to be least assertive would be his arrest, trial, passion, and crucifixion. But even at this time, he is portrayed as the predominant influence in the events he is undergoing. Although he is denied, betrayed, shackled, blindfolded, mocked, spat upon, whipped, stripped, and killed, he never appears as a victim. His inner spiritual power dwarfs the external political and religious coercion. This is especially true in the Gospel of John, but it is also an element, although more muted, in the other Gospels. Jesus in chains is still Jesus.

There is a striking exchange in the Lukan trial where Jesus suddenly but subtly reverses the flow of power. The Sanhedrin is assembled and asks him if he is the Messiah. Jesus replied,

> "If I tell you, you will not believe me, and if I question you, you will not answer. This much only will I say: 'From now on, the Son of Man will have his seat at the right hand of the Power of God.'"
>
> Luke 22:67–69

This bound (and perhaps still blindfolded) man has just told them that the conversation is over. He has met them before and he knows their game. When he answers their questions, they do not believe him, and when he asks them questions, they do not answer. Dialogue is dead. What takes its place is the judgment of the suffering one (the Son of Man) who exercises the power of God. This happens "from now on." Jesus is telling them that they will make him suffer and that this suffering, even as they inflict it, will be a judgment on them. They will not have to await sentencing. His sentencing will be their own. The one on trial puts them on trial; the one judged becomes the judge.

The outcome of this powerful "inner to outer" way of living is that Jesus is an explosive power that must be reckoned with. He is a force because the Kingdom he proclaimed and served is a force. It is like leaven which is active in an incredible amount of flour (three measures) but manages to work through it all. Or it is a seed that breaks ground, sprouts, produces first a blade, then the ear, and finally ripe wheat in the ear—even while everyone sleeps. And the people who live out of this spiritual energy go with the flow and invest their talents rather than bury them. If, as Origen suggested, Jesus is the "Kingdom himself," then he will manifest the inevitable power of seed and leaven and refuse to bury anything (Mt. 25:14–30).

Care

In itself, this inner dynamism could be mistaken for sheer exhaustible energy, powerful and unyielding but diffuse and without clear direction—a stallion in an open pasture. But the portrait of this energized Jesus is that he is a man of care. His care, which is the second aspect of our literary portrait, makes him hyper-attentive to what people say and do, fuels an unrelenting passion to heal, urges him to compassionately share the blessings and curses of creation, promotes the courage of unlimited forgiveness, and engenders an anger which is not righteous but the way great love grieves. These qualities comprise Jesus' capacity to care.

Jesus enjoined people to be attentive, and in doing so, he made some strange anatomical connections:

> 'Listen as you will, you shall not understand;
> look intently as you will, you shall not see.
> Sluggish indeed is this people's heart.
> They have scarcely heard with their ears,
> they have firmly closed their eyes;
> otherwise they might see with their eyes,
> and hear with their ears,
> and understand with their hearts . . . '
>
> Matthew 13:14–15

The eye and the ear were connected to the heart, and together they produced the spiritual ability to perceive the truth of situations. This sight and hearing which Jesus urged on others he himself had. That is the essence of the praise from Gerard Manley Hopkins which opened this chapter: "Ah! there was a heart right!/There was single eye!"

As the command to open eyes and ears came from a man wide-eyed and open-eared, the command to stay awake came from a sleepless man. The sleeping miss the moment when the master arrives (Mk. 13:33–37; Lk. 12:35–38), succumb to temptation (Lk. 22:46; Mk. 14:32–42), and their torches go out (Mt. 25:1–13). Jesus was a wide-awake man in a world gone to sleep. The prerequisite of care is noticing, and noticing demands a watching person with eyes sharp and ears alert.

Jesus is attentive. He notices short people in tall trees (Lk. 19:1–5); the humble, furtive hand of a widow by the coffers

(Mk. 12:41–42); the hunger of a twelve-year-old girl come back from the sleep of the dead (Mk. 5:43); unimportant street children shoved away (Mk. 10:13); a cry for pity from the perimeter of the crowd (Mk. 10:46–52); a pledge of loyalty which is really a boast (Lk. 22:33); a trap baited with flattery (Lk. 20:21); a woman's theological observation that avoids a personal response (Jn. 4:19); and a touch on his cloak that is different from all the rest, a touch which communicates a little more panic, a little more pleading, a touch of twelve-years' bleeding (Mk. 5:25–34).

Jesus' storytelling also reveals a keen eye and a finely tuned ear. Jesus does not tell either mythic stories of God or great adventures of heroes and heroines. His stories are about everyday people in everyday situations. He has obviously been with these people, and out of the stuff of their lives, he created the parables about life in the Kingdom.

He can catch the panicked thinking of an about-to-be fired steward (Lk. 16:1–7) and produce a wonderful parody of a proud man thanking God for his own perfection (Lk. 18:10–14). He can suggest the endless waiting of a father with a simple description:"While he was still a long way off, his father caught sight of him" (Lk. 15:20). A sturdy shepherd capable of shouldering a sheep (Lk. 15:4–6); a bustling, mad-at-herself housewife with a whirlwind broom (Lk. 15:8–9); a yawning doorkeeper waiting for his tipsy master (Lk. 12:35–38); an overseer who takes a chance and revels while his master tarries (Mt. 24:48–50); a too-prudent-for-his-own-good servant (Mt. 25:14–30); grumbling workers who kick the dirt outside the pay office (Mt. 20:1–13); a smooth son who says what his father wants to hear and a brash one who speaks his mind and then thinks the better of it (Mt. 21:28–31)—all these characters are imaginative constructions born of spiritual attentiveness. Jesus did not miss much.

This portrait of sensitivity means that Jesus lives without anesthesia. He is numb neither to the joy nor the pain of the world. Part of the strangeness of his character is that he has not developed defenses to keep both happiness and sorrow moderate. Therefore, he appears to party too quickly and excessively and to cry out too often and too vehemently.

When what is lost is found, the characters in the stories insist on a party, a party which he assures us goes on in heaven as well as on earth (Lk. 15:1–32). But we may smile and say, "What's the big fuss?" And when he comes upon an "acceptable level" of corruption in priests, lawyers, and leaders, he ties a whip of knots, either literally or with his tongue. But we may shrug and say, "So what's new?"

In the middle of events in which most people yawn, Jesus leaps with joy or bursts with anger. Quite simply, this man has not adjusted. His care makes him receive each moment as if it were the only moment. He does not suffer from world-weariness.

From whence comes this sensitivity? Perhaps we can get a clue from a remark that Abraham Maslow made after a near-fatal heart attack:

One very important aspect of the post-mortem life is that everything gets precious, gets piercingly important. You get stabbed by things, by flowers and by babies and by beautiful things—just the very act of living, of walking and breathing and eating and having friends and chatting. Everything seems to look more beautiful rather than less, and one gets the much-intensified sense of miracles.[18]

What happens when we have a death scare is that the life we took for granted and thought was guaranteed is shown to be a fragile gift. We appreciate, at least for a short time, the fact that all things are given and we see them in their radiant individuality. It is like we are seeing them for the first time.

What formerly was monotonous and repetitious is now startlingly new. Chesterton has whimsically pointed this out:

It may not be automatic necessity that makes all daisies alike; it may be that God makes every daisy separately, but never got tired of making them. It may be that He has the eternal appetite of infancy; for we have sinned and grown old, and our Father is younger than we. The repetition in Nature may not be a mere recurrence; it may be a theatrical encore.[19]

When we have this sensitivity, we say we are alive; and we mean more than that we are still breathing.

This sensitivity to everything as new was part of Jesus' make-up. Every time he breathed in, he was conscious that God had breathed out. Nothing was solid, automatic, necessary. At every moment, everything came from the love of God. Jesus never took his life for granted but at each moment received it as a free gift from his father. Therefore, he was continually "stabbed" by the beauty of the world. The nameless gratitude which we feel after a narrow escape from injury or death, Jesus felt each morning as he rose from sleep. He was a man with his arms open and his chest uncovered and so the wild world, gift of his prodigal father, leapt into his eyes and ears and joyously invaded his heart.

But this care of Jesus which is so openly receptive is in no way passive. No sooner does it receive than it engages. It moves, attacks, embraces, pursues. This care issues in a fierce desire to heal. A leper says to Jesus, "If you will to do it, you can cure me." Jesus responds: "Of course, I will it!" Everything rides on the "of course." The leper and Jesus share the same concern—his well-being. The leper knows that he is interested in his own health, but he cannot be sure of Jesus' interest. If he is concerned, he can do it, but he may not be concerned. The real revelation of this episode is not so much the power to heal but the desire to heal. The human heart has always surmised there is a power capable of mending what is broken. The doubt has always been about its interest in doing so. The man may be cured or he may not be cured, but leave no doubt about the mind of Jesus: "Of course I do!"

This overflow of care into the desire to heal suffuses the portrait of Jesus. He is pictured as a man seeking out the sick and possessed. But, once word gets around, they seek him out. Often someone comes to him with a request to come and heal or exorcise someone he or she loves. Jesus is on his feet and walking with them (Mk 5:24; Lk 7:6). More often, if they can, they come themselves: "Before long the whole town was gathered outside the door" (Mk. 1:33).

We get the sense he is flooded. They push toward him seeking to touch him (Mk. 3:10); they crowd into the house making it impossible for him to eat (Mk. 3:20). But we do not sense that this is the story of a powerful wonder worker bothered by favor-seekers, pawed and clawed by the unfortunate, reluctantly doing what he can and secretly trying to get away. They may approach him, but the impression is that he was waiting for them. While they were looking for him, he was seeking them.

The care of Jesus is sustained by compassion and forgiveness. Compassion is the experience of feeling the other's life as one's own. Three of Jesus' most powerful stories turn on the experience of compassion. The Samaritan looks on the man in the ditch with compassion and an action occurs that changes the world of the story and the world of the listeners to the story (Lk. 10:30–35). The father looks at his son with compassion and an action occurs that changes the world of the story and the world of the listeners (Lk. 15:11–32). The king looks on the servant with compassion and an action occurs which changes the world of the story and the world of the listeners (Mt. 18:21–35). Compassion is the dynamism of new and unforeseen actions which change the shape of things.

It is often noted that the Greek word for compassion indicates a movement that wells up from the deepest center of the person.[20] It suggests a response so powerful that it overflows into action. It does not specify what the action should be, but since it flows from that part of the person in touch with the divine, the action will be creative and effective. Compassion is the feeling-perception which emerges from the empathic center where God, the self, and the neighbor join. It is so great that it does not stop at the feeling of solidarity but galvanizes the person into works of solidarity.

People petition Jesus to feel this compassion toward them (Mt. 9:27; Mk. 10:47; Lk. 17:13). And since Jesus responds with power, it seems that their asking was answered. But we are also explicitly told that Jesus feels and acts out of compassion. When he sees people who are like sheep without a shepherd (Mk 6:34; Mt. 9:36), when he sees the sick (Mt. 14:14), when he meets hungry people (Mt. 15:32; Mk. 8:1), when a leper petitions him (Mk. 1:41), and when he sees a widow walking in the funeral procession of her son (Lk. 7:13), he is "moved by pity."

This empathic presence of Jesus extends beyond the human world into the world of nature. He identifies himself with light, for when people are with him, they see (Jn. 8:12); with water, for when people are with him, their thirst is slaked (Jn. 4:14); and with bread, for when people are with him, their hunger is filled (Lk. 22:19). He urges people to feel with the ravens the way the air holds them in flight and to enter into the flowers who are unself-consciously beautiful (Mt. 6:26).

Jesus wants people to participate in the frustration of a tree which cannot bear fruit (Lk. 13:6–9) and a seed that finds no reception (Mk. 4:13–20). He thinks that when enemies stand side by side and become the same sun which sears them and the same rain which drenches them, they will know the same Father who loves them (Mt. 5:44–46). He understands the created world as energized by divine presence, and so he uses the natural world as an analogy for the reception and rejection of the divine in the human world.

In the stories of Jesus, there is a very close link between compassion and forgiveness. In the three stories where compassion is the inner experience of the characters, the outer expression is forgiveness. Once the prodigal father and the king experience compassion, they are moved to forgive the son and the servant, and the lawyer who heard the story of the compassionate Samaritan construes his action not merely in terms of help but in terms of mercy. Since it is assumed that the man in the ditch is a Jew and, more precisely, is the listening lawyer himself, the Samaritan has to overcome the history of hostility between them.[21] His care flows from his ability to forgive and to get beyond racial hatred. It must be stressed that the father, the king, and the Samaritan have been wronged by the people they forgive and help. There is something in the experience of compassion that facilitates the most difficult and yet the most creative of all human actions—heartfelt forgiveness.

The experience of compassion toward those who offend us binds us to those people in such a way that forgiveness rather than retaliation becomes a possibility. In compassion, we share the world of the other at a personal depth. We do not become the other, but we are in communion with the person of the other. This means that the other person is not just his or her ideas, attitudes, or behaviors. We are in "heart-to-heart" contact. We share the space where good and evil struggle; where infinite aspirations and finite achievements clash; where, as Paul would have it, "I do, not the good I will to do, but the evil I do not intend" (Rm. 7:19). In compassion, we enter the secret chamber of the mysterious other. We discover the place where our enemy cries.

This sudden union with the other who has offended us has a powerful effect. It rids us of superiority. The commands of Jesus not to judge and not to condemn do not seem like alien dictates. We cannot judge and we cannot condemn not simply because we do not know the "whole story." That is always the case. But in the blinding exchange at the center of compassion, we found out that we, too, are offenders.

This revelation is not just a general conviction of sinfulness. It is immediate to this concrete encounter with this particular person who has offended us. What we see, if only for an instant, is that as they have reduced us to an enemy in order to strike, we have reduced them to an enemy in order to strike back. We cannot simply play the innocent offended one. We are more the same than different. In the movie *Ben-Hur,* Judah has nurtured a life-long and, by any standards other than Jesus', a justified vengeance toward Messala. When he finally kills him, the woman he loves says the deepest truth: "It is like you are become Messala."

The recognition of common sinfulness may bring a reconciliation that evades the illusion of virtue. This is Jesus' strategy with the woman taken in adultery (Jn. 8:1–11). "Let the man among you who has no sin be the first to cast a stone at her" binds them to her in the common experience of fault. Acknowledgment of their sinfulness pushes them to a mercy their pretense of purity would not allow them. More than any other episode in the Gospels, this story catches the way virtue breeds violence and the way truth brings, if not peace, than the lessening of aggression. It also sharpens the knife of Jesus' cutting advice:

> "How can you say to your brother [or sister], 'Let me take that speck out of your eye,' while all the time the plank remains in your own? You hypocrite! Remove the plank from your own eye first; then you will see clearly to take the speck from your brother's [and sister's] eye."
>
> Matthew 7:4–6

Compassion engenders a radical vision of a common humanity united by the experiences of fault and forgiveness.

The result of the experience of compassion is a bond between the offender and the one offended. This bond is deeper than the actual offense, and it is the reality of this bond that the one offended allows to influence her when she forgives the offender. Forgiveness refuses to allow the offense to be the basis of the relationship. This does not mean that the offense is not serious, but it does mean that in the mind of the one offended it is not ultimate. The one offended is not passively enduring the offense and doggedly refusing to retaliate. The one offended is actively responding to a reality that binds her to the offender more powerfully than the offense alienates her. In a world where retribution is second-nature, forgiveness is strenuous counteractivity.

Jesus contrasts responding "in kind" with responding "out of kind," and the sharp way he states it tells us something about these self-perpetuating processes:

> "You have heard the commandment, 'An eye for an eye, a tooth for a tooth.' But what I say to you is: offer no resistance to injury. When a person strikes you on the right cheek, turn and offer him the other."
>
> Matthew 5:38–39

Since the way of forgiveness seems impossible, it is helpful to consider the alternatives. It is not just an eye for an eye; it is an eye for an eye for an eye for an eye for an eye . . . Violence is self-perpetuating. The ultimate irony and evil of sin is that it turns its victims into sinners themselves. When we retaliate to the injury done to us, we make that injury the lord of our lives and act in accordance with its vengeful wishes. We are slaves to sin. There is no way out, and each time we give back "payment in kind," "payment in kind" is given back to us. When the instinct to retribution is obeyed, there is no future, only the endless repetition of the past.

Forgiving . . . is the only reaction which does not merely react but acts anew and unexpectedly, unconditioned by the act which provoked it and therefore freeing from its consequences both the one who forgives and the one who is forgiven.[22]

Forgiveness, everlasting and absolute, is the only way out of the spiral of violence.

In the gospel portrait, Jesus' stories and teaching about forgiveness are matched by his actions. He forgives his disciples their continual obtuseness and final betrayal, and from the cross, he forgives those who have crucified him. But the major emphasis is not on Jesus' forgiving those who have offended him. Rather, Jesus is the one who offers divine forgiveness to all who have sinned. It is this experience of divine compassion and forgiveness mediated through Jesus which is the energy of inter-human forgiveness. This connection is reflected in the tightly linked verses of Jesus' teaching:

> Be compassionate, as your Father is compassionate.
> Do not judge, and you will not be judged.
> Do not condemn, and you will not be condemned.
> Pardon, and you shall be pardoned.
> Give, and it shall be given to you.
>
> Luke 6:36–38

This is more than merely an exhortation to imitate God. It suggests that the experience of divine compassion initiates a way of being human. This way of being human shuns judgment and condemnation and promotes forgiveness and giving. Jesus hoped to initiate a spiral of forgiveness just as self-perpetuating as the spiral of violence.

The dynamic of Jesus' spiral begins with divine compassion forging an unbreakable bond with the human person. In the Hebrew Scriptures, this is the covenant relationship, and it is this relationship which Jesus' life and teaching radicalize. When the human partner breaks the relationship, God does not respond in kind. Divine reality focuses on the compassionate bonding, forgives the offense, and offers a renewed relationship.

This is how God relates to all humanity. It is not that some live unrighteously and need mercy, and others live righteously and require only justice. Once anger at our brother or sister is liable to the same judgment as murder and lustful looks are equivalent to adultery, we have all sinned (Mt. 5:21–22, 28). Therefore, all live by the forgiveness of God.

Our response to divine forgiveness is gratitude, praise, and an ongoing life of openness to God. But how do we stay open to God? The primary way is to extend forgiveness to others, especially to others who have offended us. To give as we have received is the dynamic of Jesus' spirituality. We have received from One we have offended. Therefore, we give to ones who offend us.

If we do this, we enter more deeply into our own experience of forgiveness which is the foundation of our selfhood. If we refuse to extend on the inter-human level what we have received on the divine-human level, we close off our life-giving experience of divine forgiveness. This is the fate of the servant who was forgiven but who did not forgive in turn (Mt.

18:21–35). It is also the deepest meaning of the petition in the Our Father "forgive us as we forgive those who trespass against us" (Lk. 11:2–4). This dynamic of giving and receiving is also at the heart of one of Jesus' most puzzling remarks: "To those who have, more will be given; from those who have not, what little they have will be taken away" (Mk. 4:25).

But what if the forgiveness extended to others is not received? What if it is perceived as weakness or foolishness and just becomes the raw material for further offenses and more elaborate exploitation? Forgiveness is ultimately an act of faith in the fundamental goodness of the human person and solicits his or her capacity to respond differently. But what if evil has such a hold on the person that the offer of a reconciliation sustained by love holds no attraction? Is it not then time to respond in kind? Why be a victim of evil?

At this crunch point the spirituality of Jesus holds adamantly to two insights. First, revenge breaks the spiral of forgiveness and contributes to the spiral of violence. Beelzebub cannot cast out Beelzebub. This is the hardest of all sayings, the one that never ceases to rub against the grain. We do not realize how radical it is until we realize how absolutely wrongheaded are the questions "Who is my neighbor?" and "How many times should I forgive my brother and sister—seven?" Both these questions presuppose limits to the extension of love and, therefore, predict a future situation where forgiveness will give way to retribution. At that moment, the spiral of forgiveness gives way to the spiral of violence.

Second, for forgiven people, extending forgiveness is a matter of enacting their identity. The foundation of their selfhood is an experience of forgiveness, and if they are to faithful to that self, they must allow it expression. This expression of the true spiritual self may imperil the bodily self. The adage "Grace may be free but it is not cheap" is a truth that the followers of Jesus know only too well. In these circumstances, the paradoxical teaching of Jesus is lucid: "Whoever would save his [her] life will lose it, but whoever loses his [her] life for my sake will find it" (Mt. 16:25).

Although the care of Jesus is revealed in his compassion and forgiveness, it has a harsher embodiment in his determination to eliminate evil and in his anger at sin. When the clean spirit in a man shrieked at Jesus, "Have you come to destroy us?" Jesus rebuked him sharply: "Be quiet! Come out of the man!" (Mk. 1:24–25). The answer to the demon's question is "Yes!" At another point, Jesus portrays himself as a thief.

> "No one can enter a strong man's house and despoil his property unless he has first put him under restraint. Only then can he plunder his house."
>
> Mark 3:27

There is no doubt that Jesus is the invader, Satan the strong owner, and people the "liberated" property. Jesus has set himself squarely at odds with the forces of evil.

Jesus is also a man of anger. He denounces oppression, unmasks all forms of hypocrisy, and threatens people with damnation. He is not sanguine about the lack of response to this offer of divine forgiveness and human reconciliation. But he does not fall under his own sanction of hating his brother and sister. What he hates is their blindness and stupidity.

For Jesus, sin is often a form of foolishness, a stupidity born of being blind and deaf to what really matters and what will ultimately be victorious. In Jesus' tirades against the religious leaders of his day, we get the impression that he could have ended each attack with "But don't you see . . . ?" As Jon Sobrino has pointed out, Jesus is paradoxically in favor of the people he attacks. "It is a paradoxical form of love, offering them salvation by destroying them as sinners."[23]

This is poignantly evident in Jesus' long harangue in the twenty-third chapter of Matthew. In this speech, the invective is unending. The leaders are vain hypocrites, frauds, blind guides, fools, a brood of serpents, a viper's nest, and there is no shortage of examples to back up each charge. But it seems that this angry man breaks down at the end and reveals his tirade as an outburst of grief. "How often have I yearned to gather your children, as a mother bird gathers her young under her wings, but you refused me" (Mt. 23:37). The real energy of his anger is his ardent desire to save them. His real pain is their refusal. He does not hate them. He is trying to get through to them.

Care is the content of Jesus' inner dynamism. Although we can talk about care as a quality of spirit, it is always concretely realized. The man of care is attentive to where he is at and who he is with. When he is confronted with suffering, he puts forth an all-out effort to heal. He is in basic sympathy with people and nature.

This sympathetic bond, energized by God's sympathetic bond with him, is the strongest reality Jesus knows, the bond he will never sacrifice. This double bond entails the mutual receiving and giving of forgiveness which is the only way it can flourish in a world of sin. Finally, his care bursts out in anger at the blindness and stupidity of people and hopes by sheer power of shock to bring them to their senses.

Freedom

In the synoptic Gospels, Jesus quotes Isaiah that he was sent to proclaim liberty to captives (Lk. 4:18). But other than this, freedom is not a major theme of Jesus' preaching or a term used to describe him or his activity. Yet freedom is a category that many feel sums up the entire Jesus phenomenon.[24]

Jesus can best be understood in terms of "freedom contrasts." His words and deeds offered freedom from the power of Satan, from crippling disease, from debilitating worry, from ego-centered striving, from burdensome religious obligations, from imprisonment to social categories, from economic hardship. The reverse side was a freedom for obedience to God's rule, for bodily health, for a life of trust, for other-centered concerns, for true worship, for genuine encounters with people, and for more just economic order. Jesus' presence was liberating in the physical, interpersonal, social, and spiritual realms.

Of course, this freedom which Jesus offered he was "in himself." The tradition has summed it up neatly: "like us in all things, save sin." Jesus is the person who is free from sin. There is no distance or guilt in his relationship to God. He lives in intimacy with God and at every moment receives his being from God. Sebastian Moore suggests that freedom from sin in relationship to God would mean that the "sense of 'I am not alone' would be overpowering. There would be an almost inconceivable flourishing of the human person."[25]

There would also be an intimacy with other people. The neighbor would not be confined to a few, and this sinless person would not leap back in self-protection or leap forward in violence. A freedom from sin is a freedom for a free-flowing relationship with God and people. James Breech says about Jesus that he was the type "that neither felt superior to others nor inferior to an absolute."[26]

There is one comparison that Jesus used which highlights both his own freedom and the resentment it triggered in other people.[27] Jesus compares people to children who whine that "we piped you a tune but you did not dance,/we sang you a dirge but you did not wail" (Lk. 7:31–34; Mt. 11:16–19). In other words, both John the Baptist and Jesus are out of step, they will not play the game the "children" have petulantly dictated. They have refused to live within the boundaries which the group has established and vigilantly guards.

Although John the Baptist came "neither eating or drinking" and Jesus came "eating and drinking," both receive the same treatment. John the Baptist is called mad, and Jesus is reduced to a drunkard and a glutton. Both are slandered because both are free to live beyond the circumscribed norms of the group—one in abstinence and the other in abundance. As long as no one is outside the group, its self-slavery goes unnoticed. But when one man dances free, the rest look at their shackled feet. The situation is ripe for the decision of freedom or slavery. We either defend the shackles or risk the dance.

The galling freedom of Jesus was most evident in his startling original responses. He was the timely person. What he said and what he did came from how he perceived the situation he was in and not from a prescribed code of behavior. He did not consult what "the right thing to do" was. Whatever he did was the right thing. He could praise a scribe as "not far from the reign of God" (Mk. 12:34) and excoriate the man who just proclaimed him as the Son of God as Satan (Mt. 16:23).

Jesus could tell a widow not to weep for her dead son (Lk. 7:13) and other mothers to weep and wish they had never given birth (Lk. 23:28–29). He could be filled with desire to eat a meal (Lk. 22:15) and with the desire to set a fire on the earth (Lk. 12:49). He allows one woman to cry on his feet and anoint him with perfume (Lk. 7:38) and tells another not to cling to him (Jn. 20:17).

Faced with the death of Lazarus, Jesus is calmly confident: "Our beloved Lazarus has fallen asleep, but I am going here to wake him" (Jn. 11:11). Faced with the death of the Baptist, "he withdrew by boat from there to a deserted place by himself"

(Mt. 14:13). Faced with his own death, "he began to be filled with fear and distress" (Mk. 14:34). Jesus was a tuning fork to the hum of each encounter, and since each encounter is unique, each response is original.

Another remarkable aspect of Jesus' freedom is his reluctance to cling. This is celebrated in the famous hymn of the Epistle to the Philippians (2:6–11):

> Though he was in the form of God,
> he did not deem equality with God
> something to be grasped at.
>
> Philippians 2:6

In fact, he did not seem to grasp at anything. Jesus was a man renowned for his preaching, healing, and his mediation of divine forgiveness. If he would keep the secret of these activities, he would maintain his superior position. Yet he trains his disciples to preach and heal and sends them out as soon as they are ready (Lk. 9:1–2). He also suggests that through their ministries God will forgive sins (Mt. 16:19; Jn. 20:22–23). He hands over the very powers that distinguish him as extraordinary, and the Johannine Christ roes so far as to say that

> whoever who has faith in me
> will do the works I do,
> and greater far than these.
>
> John 14:12

As the man breaks bread and passes it, so Jesus breaks his powers and distributes them.

But Jesus' nonclinging is total. It is not just his powers that he does not grasp at but his very life. In the synoptics it is Jesus who insists that he will suffer and die, even though his friends resist and even deny it (Mt. 16:21–23). The Johannine Christ says that no one takes his life from him but that he freely lays it down (Jn. 10:18). The reason no one can take it from him is that he never held onto it in the first place. They cannot take from Jesus what he is not clutching. This radical detachment of Jesus makes him dangerous, for as every ruler knows, the person with nothing to lose is free to speak the truth.

The detachment of Jesus from his own powers and his own life is the flip side of a radical attachment. Jesus' first act of freedom was to hand himself over to the reality he calls so directly and intimately "Abba!" This forms his identity, and identity is the necessary previous factor in all freedom.[28] The free act is not the act which is stripped of all outside influence. All human action takes place in a swirl of influences. The free act is the act that expresses the true identity of the person.

Jesus gives away his powers and hands himself over to death not in spite of the fact that he is the Son of God but because of it. This is the ultimate freedom to dispose of yourself in a way that is true to yourself. And since for Jesus the truth about him is that he is the Son of the Father, his freedom is most perfectly expressed on the cross. He hands his spirit completely over to his Father and forgives those who are executing him (Lk. 23:34, 46). He died as he lived: the free man.

The Claim

When we weave together the historical and literary portrait, is there enough fascination with this life to create desire? Do we feel emerging from the story of Jesus a claim that, if we ignore it, we may be the poorer for it?

Is there something desirable about being so at home with our own dignity that we do not have to claim it at each moment? Is the possibility that we can be all that we can be without making others less than they are worth striving for?

Would we rather be able to integrate our diminishments and eventual death into the purpose of our lives or resent them as the brutal interruptions of our plans? Would we delight if, at least once, we could break down the constricted roles which predetermine who we are and who others must be?

What if we were born apostles? What if we frantically did not have to get something out of life but sensed we were sent, our lives contributing to a larger purpose? What would life be like if we could get out of ourselves long enough to be attentive, compassionate, and forgiving? If we did not cling to who we are and what we have, would we be free to be who we are and enjoy what we have?

These might be some of the attractions which call to us from the Jesus story. As we watch him relate to life in his strange and creative way, we become aware that there are many ways of being human. It is not just that there is a diversity of work and lifestyles. There are different ways of "being," options about how to dwell upon this earth. Everyone breathes, but not everyone breathes the same way. If the way Jesus receives and gives out breath makes us turn our heads and ask "Where do you live?" then we have been claimed, and the quest is on. Franz Josef van Beeck asks the key question of the quest:

> What is it that animates this man to stand so long sufferingly firm in his kindly determination to welcome all that is human into his person and thus graciously create in his person the medium where all that is human is reconciled and opened to a life beyond all borderlines and definitions, including thc bounds of death?[29]

With this question we move explicitly to Jesus' relationship to God (the vertical dimension of faith). This is the secret energy of his liberated life and the power we wish to participate in. And Jesus is only too happy to introduce us to that power for "I came that they might have life and have it to the full" (Jn. 10:10).

But, of course, it is seldom that smooth. Some people hear the claim that comes from the story of Jesus in stark and powerful ways, and they reject it. This is the case of Flannery O'Connor's character The Misfit in "A Good Man Is Hard to Find."

"Jesus was the only One that ever raised the dead," The Misfit continued, "and He shouldn't have done it. He thrown everything off balance. If he did what He said, then it's nothing for you to do but throw away everything and follow Him, and if He didn't, than it's nothing for you to do but enjoy the few minutes you got left the best way you can—by killing somebody or burning down his house or doing some other meanness to him. No pleasure but meanness," he said and his voice had become almost a snarl.[30]

The Misfit sees it clearly, and immersed in the mysteries of freedom and iniquity, he chooses against Jesus. If the author of John were here to comment, he would nod and say, "He chose the darkness because his deeds were dark" (Jn. 3:19).

Most of us do not hear the claim so clearly or respond so wholeheartedly, even if wrongheartedly. We vacillate, not beyond envy and not completely given over to desire. As we suggested in Chapter One, we can be fascinated by a person who communicates the fullness of life and at the same time feel diminished by that fullness and seek to discredit it. Envy drives us to undercut any fullness of life which exposes our own emptiness. Envy has a million loves, but it excels, to paraphrase Eliot, at saying the right things for the wrong reasons. In regard to the Jesus story, envy often uses orthodoxy in an inconsistent way for very consistent purpose.

On the one hand, envy insists on the full divinity of Jesus. It will settle for no less. This means that the claim of Jesus flows from the fact he is God. We owe him a response of worship and obedience. What is important about him is not the life he led but the divine reality he was. The key text is the prologue of John: the Word was God and the Word became flesh. Jesus is reduced to his divine origins.

On the other hand, envy insists on the full humanity of Jesus. It will settle for no less. Jesus was a first-century Jew and subject to the limitations of space and time like anyone else. The key text is "Is this not the carpenter, the son of Mary, a brother of James and Joses and Judas and Simon?" (Mk. 6:3). Jesus is reduced to his human origins.

In the age of suspicion, we should ask not only if both these perspectives are faithful to the tradition but how they are functioning in the lives of people who hold them. The divine Jesus never quite touches the earth, and the human Jesus cannot transcend it. One lives in the inaccessible sky, and the other lives in the inaccessible past. We cannot follow one because he is the Son of God in such a way that his humanity is a total exemption. We cannot follow the other because he is so culture-bound to the first century that he cannot speak our language. We have a Jesus who is true God and true Man, but never master. Envy is afraid of what it desires, and so it uses its genius to make the desirable unattainable.

But this envious twisting of Christology does play upon a real fear at the heart of the desire to apprentice ourselves to the life of Jesus. When we are about to enter into the mystery of the human and the divine, fear always mixes with fascination. For Rudolph Otto it was the very definition of religious experience: "*mysterium tremendum et fascinans.*"

The divine-human offer as it shines through the person of Jesus of Nazareth fascinates and terrifies us. It is all that our hearts have ever wanted and all that our hearts have ever feared. It is the fulfillment of the promise of our bones and the embrace we fear will engulf us. We rejoice that we are at the place where life lost is life gained, and we fear we may be at the place where life lost is just life lost.

What exactly is it that we fear? Three artists may give us some clues. T. S. Eliot's last lines of "The Journey of the Magi" give us one man's bittersweet reaction to an encounter with Christ:

All this was a long time ago, I remember,
And I would do it again, but set down
This set down
This: were we led all that way for
Birth or Death? There was a Birth, certainly,
We had evidence and no doubt. I had seen birth and death,
But had thought they were different; this Birth was
Hard and bitter agony for us, like Death, our death.
We returned to our places, these Kingdoms,
But no longer at ease here, in the old dispensation,
With an alien people clutching their gods.
I should be glad of another death.[31]

A second less-than-enthusiastic presentation of Jesus comes from Hazel Motes, the protagonist of Flannery O'Connor's *Wise Blood.* He knows the perils of an invitation from Christ:

Later he saw Jesus move from tree to tree in the back of his mind, a wild ragged figure motioning him to turn around and come off into the dark, where he was not sure of his footing, where he might be walking on water and not know it, and then suddenly know it and drown.[32]

These two reflections focus our fear. We are afraid that Jesus will make us a stranger to our comforts; make the life we now lead an "old dispensation"; and take us, without our knowing it, into a life that will be too much for us, into water over our heads where we may drown. Quite simply, the attraction might prove fatal to the life we now find rather comfortable.

But it is Annie Dillard who uncovers the heart of our hesitation. She begins her wonderful autobiographical reflection "God in the Doorway," with the memory of a past Christmas. One Christmas Eve, Santa Claus "stood in he doorway with night over his shoulder." He had come to visit, but young Annie would have none of it. She ran upstairs and refused to come down.

Santa Claus was an old man whom you never saw, but who nevertheless saw you; he knew when you'd been bad or good. He knew when you'd been bad or good! And I had been bad.[33]

She goes on to reflect that this Santa Claus was really a "rigged-up" Miss White who lived across the street. Miss White meant "no harm on earth," but Annie remembers another time she ran from her. It was on a summer day in the yard. Miss White had a magnifying glass and focused a 'dab of sunshine" on her palm. It burned and she ran and did not look back. Annie Dillard concludes her essay with this penetrating insight:

Even now I wonder: if I meet God, will he take and hold my bare hand in his, and focus his eye on my palm, and kindle that spot and let me burn?

But no. It is I who misunderstood everything and let everybody down. Miss White, God, I am sorry I ran from you. I am still running, running from that knowledge, that eye, that love from which there is no refuge. For you meant only love, and love, and I felt only fear, and pain. So once in Israel love came to us incarnate, stood in the stoodway between two worlds, and we were all afraid.[34]

This is the ultimate reason why we fear the desire in us created by the person of Jesus. He invites us into an experience of all-knowing love which is beyond our control and comprehension.

So we are brought to the point of responding to the claim, following our desires, and confronting our fears. Is there anything which will get us "over the hump"? Is there some insight which will allow desire to overcome fear and to push us down the road with Jesus? Karl Rahner has a helpful philosophic consideration:

One must have reasonable grounds for abandoning oneself to another—for committing, for entrusting oneself to another. And yet, in this self-abandonment, once all antecedent considerations, verifications and demands of reasonableness and legitimation are posited—one ventures more, and must venture more, than these grounds seem to justify.[35]

It seems the operative word is—*leap*.

But there is also a story that might show us how to advance. Elkanah is married to Hannah. Hannah cannot conceive. She is deeply depressed, refuses to eat, and weeps continually. Elkanah tries to console her: "Hannah, why do you weep, and why do you refuse to eat? Why do you grieve? Am I not more to you than ten sons?" (1 Sam. 1:8). Hannah does not answer.

There comes a point in the decision to acknowledge the aim and to follow our fascination when all we are and all we have addresses us: "Are we not more to you than ten Jesuses?" And when we cannot answer, the truth begins to dawn. We may have trouble living with Jesus, but we cannot envision life without him. It is not that all we are and all we have is not good. It is good, but it is not enough, and without Jesus, we suspect it will soon go sour.

This is definitely a backdoor entry into discipleship. But what is important is that we are with Jesus, sometimes close and sometimes at a distance, but always within the sound of his voice. If we were not with him, we would be inconsolable. Could this be the experience of Holy Saturday, the day that never saw him smile? Could that be the day that those who walked with him truly knew they were disciples, the day he was not there and they could not imagine themselves without him?

Part Two

Discipleship

CHAPTER FOUR

THE SPIRIT MASTER

Hope, Life, Way, Salvation, Understanding, Wisdom, Light, Judge, Door, Most High, King, Precious Stone, Prophet, Priest, Messiah, Sabaoth, Teacher, Spouse, Mediator, Scepter, Dove, Hand, Stone, Son, Emmanuel, Vineyard, Shepherd, Sheep, Peace, Root, Vinestock, Olive Tree, Source, Wall, Lamb, Victim, Lion, Intercessor, Word, Man, Net, Rock, House: CHRIST JESUS IS EVERYTHING!

Pope Damasus

"You address me as 'Teacher' and 'Lord,'
and fittingly enough,
for that is what I am."

John 13:13

In Part One we suggested that the transmission of faith is an interpersonal event. This event is triggered by people whose perceptions, attitudes, and actions we find fascinating. If this lure is strong enough, we apprentice ourselves to these people to find the source of their power and participate in it. Jesus is such a person. His story, from birth through life and death to resurrection, is an invitation. If we accept it, we begin the process of discipleship.

This has happened. We have encountered Jesus as the One who knows how to live and die, and we want to heed the injunction of Philippians: "Your attitude must be that of Christ" (Phil. 2:5). Jesus is the embodiment and revelation of the interaction between the divine and human spirit, and it is this "mind" we want to make our own. Therefore, we address him as Spirit Master.

Earlier we stressed that although Jesus may not have used titles about himself, everyone else did. We are no exception. But if we are to use titles, we must know what role they play within a faith commitment to Jesus. And if we are to use a specific title like Spirit Master, we must probe both the meaning of *Spirit* and the meaning of *Master.* These are the concerns of this chapter.

How Titles Work

In Christian history there seems to be no shortage of images and titles for Jesus. The New Testament itself has an abundant supply—Prophet, Son of God, Good Shepherd, Messiah, Son of Man, Sower, Savior, Son of David, Lord, Second Adam, Servant, Christ, Word, and on and on. In *Jesus Through the Centuries,* Jaroslav Pelikan has traced some of the major ways Jesus has been portrayed in Western culture. At one time or another, people have named Jesus The Monk Who Rules the World, The Bridegroom of the Soul, The Universal Man, The Mirror of the Eternal, The Prince of Peace, The Poet of the Spirit, The Liberator, The Man Who Belongs to the World.[1] But for an exuberant list which leaves the reader breathless, Pope Damasus, whose images of praise opened this chapter, is not to be outdone.

Naming Jesus grows out of the process of relating contemporary experience and tradition. In the early Church, the event of Jesus was the contemporary experience and the people borrowed clues from both the Hebraic and Hellenistic traditions to interpret it. Jesus was understood in terms of the available cultural categories. The result was the storehouse of titles and images in the New Testament.

As the Christian people moved through history, a different combination of experience and tradition developed. Gradually the canon of Scripture was established and became the major interpretive tool of Christian faith. Whatever happened in the lives of Christians, they related it to the Scriptures, especially the New Testament.

Under the impact of new historical experiences, Christians selected from the richness and variety of the Scriptures perspectives that spoke to them. In this way, new aspects of the four stable stories of Jesus became prominent. A neglected passage became banner material. In short, Jesus was renamed. This renaming was generated by contemporary experience and at the same time genuinely grounded in the tradition, especially Scripture.

One way of understanding this process stresses the chameleon character of the Christ image. Christians adapt Jesus to the temper of the times. He becomes the premier citizen of the age and embodies its major values. Schweitzer is often given the credit for documenting this most convincingly:

> Each successive epoch found its own thoughts in Jesus, which was indeed, the only way in which it could make him live . . . One created him in accordance with one's own character . . . There is no historical task which so reveals someone's true self as the writing of a Life of Jesus.[2]

If the process of naming Jesus is left at this, Jesus becomes an inkblot. The titles and images of Jesus are reduced to ideological support for the dominant modes of thinking, feeling, and acting.

But there is another way to understand this image-making and title-bestowing activity of Christians. It does not deny the personal and cultural influences at work in naming Jesus, but it resituates the whole enterprise. This activity is now done within the household of faith. We do not name Jesus to find out who he is or who he must have been, given what we now know about the mysteries of God, self, society, and universe. Neither do we use him as indirect indicator of what is happening in the depths of our own being. We live within the full mystery of Jesus Christ—his historical existence, his risen glory, and his presence among us through the Spirit, and we are committed to the reality he embodies and manifests. This faith posture gives our naming of Jesus a deeper significance.

Franz Josef van Beeck explores this significance as a threefold dynamic movement.[3] First, our names for Jesus are not arbitrary. They carry our human concerns, and no matter what they are, Jesus embraces them. Nothing is automatically excluded; all our fears and desires are included. Some examples from the Gospels might be the following: Son of God carries our concern with the nature and intentions of divine reality; Son of Man (when it refers to the Book of Daniel figure) embodies our concern with the nature and criteria of ultimate judgment; Second Adam asks about the processes of re-creation; Savior wants to know about the power of sin and the way of salvation; Son of David seeks guidance on the nature of political power. Since Jesus is fully human, every concern of humanity finds a welcome in him.

Second, Jesus makes our concerns obedient to the reality he knows. The fullness of divinity in Christ makes it inevitable that our concerns are transformed through their contact with him. Acceptance is followed by purification. As we mentioned in Chapter Three when we discussed the identity of Jesus, the reality of Jesus is always more than the names we bring to him.

The titles and images tell us something about Jesus, but more importantly, Jesus redefines the titles and images. The meanings we have attached to the images and titles undergo changes when we apply them to Jesus. The title "Son of God," with whatever meanings we may have attached to it, may tell us something about Jesus, but it is the life, death, and resurrection of Jesus of Nazareth which tells us what being the Son of God means. When the titles and images are reconfigured, the life issues which we have attached to them are also changed.

My surmise is that this transformation of concerns goes on in two ways: First, the reality of Jesus sees the concerns differently. When we come to Jesus with images and titles and ask him to preside over our concerns, we have construed those concerns in a certain way and invested ourselves in them to a certain degree. The dialogue with Jesus usually leads to a new construal of the concern and either a deinvestment or reinvestment of time and energy.

Second, our concerns are limited and partial. When they contact Jesus, they enter the company of all the other concerns that have been brought to him. Our images and titles must stand side by side with other images and titles. This new context leads to seeing things in a new way. Our concerns are changed by placing them in the heart of the man who has accepted all concerns.

This is part of what the Pontifical Biblical Commission means by the "principle of totality" and "integral Christology."[4] The full, privileged witness of the Scriptures contains a host of concerns, some enduringly human and some of passing historical interest. Many of these concerns are brought to Jesus under the aegis of titles and images. Our contemporary concerns, some enduringly human and some of passing historical interest, enter into this well-rounded witness.

It would be a mistake if we considered our approach to Jesus to exhaust his truth and meaning. It is necessary for each generation of believers to bring their concerns to Jesus, but it is also necessary for the totality of concerns which constitute Scripture to talk back to each generation of believers. The relationship between experience and tradition must be a mutual dialogue.

The third moment places our accepted and transformed concerns in a perspective of hope. But it is not possible to predict in advance how this hope will come about and what exactly its contents will be. If hope could be predicted, it would merely be an extrapolation of what is presently available. It would inevitably be a desire for more of what is rather than an openness for what is not yet.

> Here, however, we must make a distinction between hope and what we can call desire. Hope is hope for we know not what. It is expectancy in face of a future which is ultimately unknown. It is certainly hope of fulfillment (otherwise it would not be hope) but we have not the first idea of what that fulfillment will turn out to be. Desire, on the other hand, takes its form and outline from what we already are . . . The object of desire is my present self with everything eliminated from it which hinders it from enjoying life. In contrast, the object of hope is a blank cheque.[5]

Gabriel Marcel suggests that hope entails "a kind of radical refusal to reckon possibilities . . . it is as though it carried with it as a postulate the assertion that reality overflows all possible reckonings."[6] We never know hope until it arrives.

The basis of our hope is the death and resurrection of Jesus, and it is that event which suggests this paradoxical dynamic—we hope without knowing the form hope will take. Historical reconstructions of the life of Jesus suggest that his major concern was the Kingdom of God. This concern was initiated and directed by God, and as it was played out, it was continually made obedient to God.

Jesus saw that the Kingdom would come not only in power through his teachings and healings but also in weakness through his suffering and death. This was the result of sinfulness, but also, ironically, it was part of the divine plan.

> "Abba, you have the power to do all things. Take this cup away from me. But let it be as you would have it, not as I."
>
> Mark 14:36

In the face of the seeming destruction of the concern which constituted his very being, Jesus maintained hope. But how he and his concern would be vindicated was not clear. Jesus entered into the dark night of trust which precedes the dawn of hope. Hope is more than the mere projection of desire.

The disciples' path to hope is even more radical and disjointed. Their concern with the Kingdom had not been fully purified by their contact with Jesus. He had tried to instruct them into the necessity of suffering and dying, but they did not understand. Since they envisioned the Kingdom largely in terms of glory, they experience Jesus' death as a complete negation of their concern. "We were hoping that he was the one . . . " say the disillusioned disciples on the road to Emmaus (Lk. 24:21).

For the disciples, the experience of the resurrection is not only the fulfillment of their concern, but it is also the beginning of understanding how their concern was transformed. They saw that Jesus "had to die," that their concern with the power of God's Kingdom had to be transformed in this way. They effectively said: "We would never have thought that is how it would have happened, but now that it has happened, we see that it could not have been otherwise." Hope is never seen coming, but once it has arrived, everything else is seen in the proper perspective.

This understanding of hope intimately interrelates the threefold dynamic, but it does not see them as a series of smooth transitions. Once the initial concerns are accepted, they are often changed in drastic ways. It may appear that what we came for has been lost. But the process has not dismissed our concerns but transfigured them.

This transfiguring provides new possibilities. But when their fulfillment arrives, it seems to come as an unexpected, if not unbidden, gift. The transformation was the preparation, but it did not then produce the result. There is a break in the process. Hope arrives on the heels of impossibility. Paradoxically put, only when all is lost is everything won.

But once hope arrives, everything falls into place. From the vantage point of fulfillment, we are able to look back and see the true nature of our original concern and understand the crucial role the transformation of that concern played. It is then we begin to speak of providence when only a short time ago we had been speaking of abandonment. It is then we speak of the value of "holding on" and of "hoping without hope" when only a short time ago we had been so tempted to let go and despair. The pain and the glory of living in time is that everything is provisional until everything is over. The truth about Jesus is known only from the perspective of resurrection.

We have come to Jesus with the hybrid title "Spirit Master." To eyes and ears that are accustomed to christological debates, this may appear to be a reductionism. The knee-jerk reaction might be: "Jesus is not just a spiritual master; he is the Son of God." But in our understanding, the various titles are not in competition. They embody different yet legitimate concerns.

Also, the fullness of the tradition—the double homoousion of Jesus (one in being) with God and humanity—is continually honored as the permeating context of the naming activity. It is precisely because of belief in the orthodox reality of Jesus that the other titles are applied to him. The multiple titles are a sign of our commitment to the God-Man and our desire to bring all life under his presidency.

Spirit Master carries our concern, simple sounding yet monumental: "Teach us how to live in relationship to God and neighbor." We can expect this concern to undergo the demanding threefold dynamic. Our concern will be wholeheartedly accepted. Yet the strange combination of fear and hope about Jesus expressed in Chapter Three—that he may take us places we do not wish to go—is never absent. Jesus relates every concern to the reality of God and neighbor he knows, and often the God and neighbor he knows is not the God and neighbor we know. Our interchange with him will undoubtedly deepen and extend our concern.

Also, our contact with Jesus, the Spirit Master, will lead us to diverse and deeper affirmations—Son of God, Liberator, Son of Man—and to the variety of concerns these titles carry. The acceptance of our concern about learning to live in relationship to God and neighbor leads inevitably to its transformation. From this process, an openness to the new will emerge. But the fulfillment will be a gift, unpredictable and surprising, as befits the nature of true hope.

The content of our concern is the relationship between the human and divine spirit or, in more specific language, the fundamental attitudes which constitute how we relate to both God and neighbor. What will happen to this concern remains to be seen. We cannot preempt the process. But the form of our concern is a request to be taught. So there is a need to bring our cultural understanding of "teaching" under some scrutiny. There may be some discrepancy between the way Jesus teaches and the way we are used to being taught. At the very least, it is wise to investigate the relational dynamics which will be at work if we apprentice ourselves to Jesus.

The Ways of The Spirit Master

We have chosen the title Spirit Master rather than Teacher of Faith. It was a judgment call. Both titles imply relationship between someone who knows and someone who does not. Their polar opposites are respectively disciple and student. Both titles need to be purified of certain cultural understandings, for certain renditions of teacher-student or master-disciple relationships will not allow us access to the way Jesus relates. Also, both titles specify the area of interaction—the area of the spiritual and the area of faith. Once again, both these words carry inappropriate connotations. Both would need to be corrected before we can begin.

In Western society, Teacher of Faith is a more available title than Spirit Master. But it has a strong and not easily dismissed connotation which is deadly to the learning style which allows access to Jesus. Teacher of Faith suggests distance and impartiality. The teacher is someone who disseminates information; in this case, a body of beliefs are passed along. He or she has mastered some subject matter and is about the business of organizing it and passing it along. The student is a secondary object of attention. As teachers often say with a shrug, students either "get the material or they don't." Most educators would immediately challenge this lopsided rendition of studentteacher relationships. But it would seem that the educational experience of many people confirms it.

The title Spirit Master initially focuses Jesus in his capacity to engage people on the level of spirit and invite them into his own spirit. He does not teach lessons; he primarily encounters people. He is passionately person-centered. When he tells his disciples to come away with him to an out-of-the-way place, he is not only suggesting rest and relaxation (Mk. 6:31). He wants time with them. Just being with his disciples is an essential ingredient of his way of teaching and their way of learning. Jesus engages the total person. In modern parlance, he communicates in the context of an "I-Thou" encounter.

Certainly Jesus instructs his disciples on the level of perceptions, attitudes, and actions. In fact, our focus will be on perceptions and attitudes. But in and through this communication, a deeper reality is handed on. The very spirit of Jesus is communicated. This happens through symbiosis and osmosis. They walk and talk and eat and work with Jesus, and there is a slow assimilation of how he sees and hears the world.

This process is partly conscious and partly unconscious. But it achieves some stability when one day a disciple makes the outrageous remark: "If Jesus were here, he would . . . " This comment is untenable on historical grounds, for the disciple is about to say something about a current situation which Jesus did not face and so did not say anything directly about it. Also it must be checked for arrogance—is it an attempt to bolster the disciple's own position by attributing it to Jesus? But when it is spoken truly, it signals something quite significant. The remark is justified because the disciple so shares the spirit of the Master that he feels confident to speak for him.

Aaron Milavec talks about this assimilation of the Master in a very helpful way:

> . . . a well-trained disciple could be relied upon to accurately and faithfully present the deepest concerns and patterns of judgment that were

> exhibited by his master. To accomplish this, the disciple did not act as a modern press reporter who observes and probes his subject. Nor did the disciple give himself to memorizing faithfully and repeating meticulously the collected discourses of his master. No. The disciple entered much more intimately into his subject than this. He roomed and roamed with him. He learned his moods, his passions, his sorrows. He learned "how he unlaced his sandals and how he laced them up again." Out of this experience, the disciple later spoke of his master as his long-time companion and his "father"—the one who shaped his life. In fact, the disciple was undoubtedly always disappointed as to how little of what he knew he could convey in words.[7]

Once the spirit is shared, the person of the Master lives on in the person of the disciple. The disciple is then in the marvelous yet frustrating position that is so simply but accurately phrased by Michael Polanyi: "He knows more than he can say."

In fact, the whole process of knowing which surrounds a Spirit Master is personal and intuitive. It is the type of knowing which brings enlightenment and is deeper than conceptual understanding. Master Yamada tells the story of an American Catholic priest who came to him and asked about the nature of enlightenment. In the course of their conversation, the priest made the connection between the "Mu" of Zen and the mind of the child in the Jesus tradition:

> Delighted, he [the American priest] slapped his thigh and said, "I understand!"
>
> "It's too soon to feel so happy. You've understood here (pointing to his head), but in Zen you have to understand here (pointing to his hara or belly)."

> "I majored in philosophy in college. If I understand up here, that's good enough."[8]

The master is not satisfied with mental connections. The disciple must experience the teaching physically and spiritually.

This gives us a clue to the depth of the relationship between Jesus the Master and anyone who would be his disciple. Jesus wants the disciple to experience the reality he knows; he does not want to pass along the conclusions of his experience. In the deepest moment, it is not a sharing of belief and theology but an introduction to Abba. If Abba is met, shared beliefs follow, flowers out of the same soil. All knowledge must be realized. Realized knowledge changes perception and overflows into action.

This distinction between belief and perception is important. John Cobb elaborates on it:

> For most men the world is very real. If they believe in God at all, they accept the idea that his reality is prior and incomparably superior to that of the world. This belief modifies their perceptions to some degree, but intellectual belief remains in some tension with perception . . . That means that what one really cares about is himself and his world, and that his real interest in God is limited largely to how he hopes or fears that God may impinge upon that world . . .
>
> For Jesus the situation was quite different. His perception conformed with his belief. Hence he could speak directly out of his perception. His preaching was not proclamation of an ought that stood over against him supported by beliefs that were heteronomously grounded. It was a description of

> what he saw from a perspective that could not be transcended. Whereas others recognized that man should live from God and for God, Jesus embodied that life.[9]

The Master wants the disciple to see so that belief is not an alien conviction, imposed from without. To get this point across, belief and seeing are often strongly contrasted. This is the case in a little story from Anthony de Mello called "Noninstruction":

> "What does your Master teach?" asked a visitor.
> "Nothing," said the disciple.
> "Then why does he give discourses?"
> "He only points the way—he teaches nothing."
> The visitor couldn't make sense out of this, so the disciple made it clearer: "If the Master were to teach, we would make beliefs out of his teachings. The Master is not concerned with what we believe—only with what we see."[10]

The real accomplishment of a Spirit Master and his disciples is to bring together belief and seeing.

Hopefully the title Spirit Master conveys this sense of personal engagement, spirit sharing, and realized understanding. However, as a title, it has its own set of difficulties. The caricature of a disciple's relationship to the master is one of blind submission. Disciples suspend all judgment and hand themselves over to the will of the master. They follow the master's directives obediently, without questioning or grumbling. The autonomy of the disciple seems to be in jeopardy. There is a thin and easily crossed line between disciple and slave. Although this is an exaggeration, there is an underlying truth in this presentation of discipleship. But it is a truth that is properly perceived only in a fuller context.

Disciples begin by trusting their intuition. They have been fascinated by a certain way of life and the underlying power that sustains it. They intuit that the one who lives this way can teach them to live in a similar way. So they apprentice themselves to the one they consider a master. If the master accepts them—and our assumption is that Jesus is open to all who sincerely seek him—they submit to a training. This training demands that they allow the master to lead them. For the moment, they must suspend critical judgment.

> You follow your master because you trust his manner of doing things even when you cannot analyze and account in detail for its effectiveness. By watching the master and emulating his efforts in the presence of his example, the apprentice unconsciously picks up the rules of the art . . . These hidden rules can be assimilated only by a person who surrenders himself to that extent uncritically to the imitation of another.[11]

If patterns of perceptions are to be changed, the master must be given a chance. If the master is criticized at every turn, the disciples are trying to accommodate the teaching to the categories they already know. They have effectively reversed the roles of master and disciple.

So there is a need for an initial surrender, a willingness to ponder the master's words and follow his directives. This surrender is not passivity. It is a psychic posture of receptivity which must be rigorously maintained. The mystery of the way of Jesus is not easy to discover and participate in.

Conversion experiences may be "big bang" events which turn us around and face us in the right direction. But discipleship is a long walk on a rough road.

> "Enter through the narrow gate. The gate that leads to damnation is wide, the road is clear, and many choose to travel it. But how narrow is the gate that leads to life, how rough the road, and how few there are who find it!
>
> Matthew 7:13–14

There are child prodigies in music and math, but in the realm of the spirit, there are only men and women of many years who have combined the openness of the child with the experience of the adult.

Many give up on discipleship to Jesus too soon. They come up against the hard sayings and the radical actions, and their common sense is offended. They cannot stomach the lilies of the field or the rubbed raw other cheek or banishing the fun of lust from the heart. These sayings are hard to endure, and they do not seem to be the words of eternal life (Cf. Jn. 6:60–69).

Our instinct is to ridicule and refute what we do not understand. We assert our own attitudes and outlooks and argue for their absolute validity. We begin to question the Master before we have found the Master's secret. We are no longer open to what is being given to us. But the advice of other disciples who have gone before us is "Hang in there!" In time, the way of Jesus will not be alien and imposed from without. It will be the full flowering of our spirit, and we will see, with that strange nonarrogant certitude of spiritual insight, that it could not be otherwise.

But if we can give up too soon, we can also hang in there too long. Our sustained receptivity must have a payoff. The disciple must meet the reality that suffuses the Master's liberated life. Some perceptual shift must occur. Surrender is not the essence of discipleship; it is merely the discipline needed to attain new insight.

The essence of discipleship is the introduction and appropriation of the power which the master has access to. The ultimate purpose of the master is not to mystify and remain permanently puzzling. The light must dawn for the disciples, their eyes must be open, their ears must be unstopped. If this is not happening, something must change in order to make it happen. Our assumption is that Jesus wants to give away his power. Discipleship is finding a way to receive it.

When we say that Jesus is the Spirit Master, another set of distinctions need to be made. In popular parlance, the spiritual often connotes flight from the world. The spiritual master lives on the mountain, breathes rarefied air, and does not fare too well when he ventures into the village.

> The holy man lived on the mountain for forty years. He meditated, fasted, and detached his soul from every vice. Finally, he was persuaded to come down from the mountain to teach his way of salvation to the people. When the Lord Krishna heard this, he transformed himself into a hulking brute and waited at the city gate. When the holy man passed through the gate, this hulking brute bumped and jostled him. The holy man raised his walking stick in anger. The brute cringed and spoke, "It is easy to be a holy man on the mountain."

The spiritual is often envisioned as a disengaged form of life that seldom succeeds when it is put to the test.

But the spirit of which Jesus is the master is not a separate entity that must be cultivated at the expense of other dimensions of the human personality. It is the hidden center and the secret energy of every dimension of life. It can be distinguished but not separated from the biological, psychological, and social.

The pervasiveness of the spiritual is imaginatively captured in Dryden's *Tempest.* "What is a soul?" Derinda asks her lover. "A small blue thing," he replies, "that runs about within us." She replies, "Then I have seen it/ In a frosty morning/ Run smoking from my Mouth." The spirit is the depth dimension of human reality and pushes outward to suffuse all of life.

This distinction-in-relationship between a spiritual depth and how it is refracted through the biological, psychological, and social dimension is important. It respects the "differentiation of consciousness" which many think is the hallmark of our secularity. We are capable of interpreting experience from many perspectives. These perspectives—biological, psychological, sociological, and spiritual—must be honored and yet related to one another. This awareness of different perspectives is concretely expressed by a woman who is a member of a catechumenate group:

> Once, when our group of catechumens was talking about God's role in our lives, someone began to describe how she prays to God for almost everything—from finding parking places to making the dishwasher work. I was quite impressed with this faith, and was prepared to admit that it was the only real faith. I also knew that it could never be mine, and wondered where that left me.
>
> But after discussions with one of the priests in our parish I came to realize that this was more a matter of temperament. Some people tend to relate everything to ultimate causes. I, on the other hand,

> who not only work as a scientist but think as one, am always looking for the most proximate causes. The religious approach of these two persons is going to be different. I have come to see that this difference is not good or bad, just different. And there is room for each of us in the Church.[12]

We are assuming the "temperament" of the woman who is the scientist. We are not approaching Jesus as a doctor (the biological dimension) or a counselor (the psychological dimension) or a politician (the social dimension), and definitely not as a dishwasher, repairman, or a finder of parking places. He is the master of the spiritual. But what he helps us discover will have biological, psychological, and political implications. These implications will be the overflow of a spiritual orientation.

One way in which the spiritual influences the other dimensions is through perceptual shift. A summary of Jesus' impact is "See, I make all things new!" (Rev. 21:5). The statement does not say that he makes new things, but that he makes all things new. This newness comes from seeing them in an original way. Jesus views the biological, psychological, and social from fundamental attitudes toward God and neighbor. This vantage point brings a freedom to appreciate, criticize, and act toward the body, the self, and society in a certain way. In a dimensional understanding of human existence, influences are mutual and interrelated. But Jesus' style is to transform the spiritual depth which changes our perception of everything else.

This distinction has another important facet. It provides the theoretical structure for Jesus' continuing relevance to the human condition. In the course of history, the precise issues on the biological, psychological, and social dimension change again and again. But the spiritual dimension, which is constituted by the fundamental relationship to God and neighbor, is a transcultural constant. This double relationship is the religious structure of human existence. The Master who initiates and develops people in these two relationships can have universal and timeless appeal.

We now have a nuanced understanding of what it means to call Jesus the Spirit Master. We are bringing to him our concern about how to live and die in relationship to God and our neighbor. We can expect a more enthusiastic welcome than we might want, a transformation we might resist, and fulfillment beyond what we might imagine.

Jesus will demand that we spend time with him, engage us personally, share his spirit, and help us perceive the world the way he does. We will have to submit to his mastery and, at least momentarily, bracket our taken-for-granted perceptions and attitudes. He will lead us into the dimension of the spirit, and when we become aware of the source he knows so well, we will see all things new.

CHAPTER FIVE

THE ART OF THE MASTER

"He looked around at them with anger."

Mark 3:5

"Then Jesus looked at him with love."

Mark 10:21

"He looked directly at them."

Luke 20:17

Jesus cannot look at us in the same way. We cannot come into direct physical contact with him. But through the gospel stories we can watch Jesus as he looks at others, listen as he talks to others, be present to him as he is present to them. And if, through the process of the imagination, we can enter into their encounter with Jesus, we will encounter him ourselves. As he exercises his art with them, drawing them into himself and through himself to the source of his power, he will be drawing us along into the same source. In short, he will look, talk, and be present to us. We become disciples to the extent that we enter into the discipleship process in the Gospels.

The four gospels are comprised of strikingly individual episodes which are united into an overall story. Both as a whole and in their parts, the Gospels can be appropriated in many different ways. Our suggestion is that when we view Jesus as the Spirit Master, many individual episodes of the overall story of Jesus yield fresh and evocative meanings. The lens of "spiritual master" allows us to see things which we may have overlooked. We no longer take it for granted that this story is about prayer or judgment or riches. It may be about the greatness and perversity of the human spirit as it stumbles about the earth praying and judging and making money. This approach may yield the insights which will teach us how to live.

But who will teach us how to read the Gospels in this way? Aaron Milavec suggests that we need contemporary Christian masters to introduce us to the perennial Master:

> When properly understood, the Scriptures present only a set of coded symbols. As such, the Scriptures are entirely mute. They are like the scores of Mozart's violin concertos: a living master is required to bring the score alive and to thrill us with the depth of aesthetic feeling that it contains. In parallel fashion, it requires a Christian master to break open the text of Scripture and to correctly nourish the messianic holiness proper to our own time.[1]

This is undoubtedly how to do it. A living faith has a chain of disciples going all the way back to the Master. These disciples share the Master's spirit and are capable of showing newcomers the intricacies of his way of life. Therefore, apprenticeship to Jesus would include the disciple, a contemporary master, and the inspired witness of the Original Master. In and through the interaction of these three, the spirit of the Original Master is present and active.

For our purposes, this means that we must gather clues from some contemporary masters. Those for whom "the scriptures have been broken open" can perhaps break them open for us. But we must be careful here. A delicate balance is required. In order to enter the text effectively, we need some perspectives, but we do not need to be so overburdened with presuppositions that all we find in the text is what we have already brought to it. C. S. Lewis has warned about an excessively aggressive attitude toward a text. "We are so busy doing things with the work that we give it too little chance to work on us. Thus increasingly we meet only ourselves."[2] This is the problem we reflected on earlier. A Jesus who is merely a mirror cannot teach us how to live.

The attitude of surrender which is necessary for a disciple is also necessary in relationship to the text a disciple would learn from. Surrender is not psychic laziness but attentive receptivity. With the use of clues from others, we gain entry into the text. But once inside the text, our psychic posture shifts, and we watch and wait patiently for the Master to teach us. For the time being, critical reason is suspended. C. S. Lewis has some valuable advice once again:

> No poem [Gospel story] will give up its secret to a reader who enters it regarding the poet as a potential deceiver, and determined not to be taken in. We must risk being taken in, if we are to get anything.[3]

The slogan is "the text must interpret the interpreter before the interpreter can interpret the text." As C. S. Lewis goes on to say: when it comes to effectively reading the Gospels "all probability is against those who attack."[4]

Therefore, we need enough clues to get into the text, but not so many that we render the text superfluous. We will explore three perspectives which will hopefully increase our sensitivity to the texts and help us become disciples of the scriptural portrait of Jesus. First, we should become familiar with the way Jesus reads hearts, for that is what he must do for us. Second, we should note some of the techniques which he uses to apprentice his contemporaries, for he will be using the same techniques on us. Third, we need to understand the limits and possibilities of third-party discipleship, for that is the position we are in.

The Reader of Hearts

The Gospels often tell us that Jesus knew what was in people's hearts. John says it straight out: "He needed no one to give him testimony about human nature. He was well aware of what was in man's heart" (Jn. 2:25). But this is not just a vague philosophic remark. The previous two verses provide the clue to what Jesus saw.

> While he was in Jerusalem during the Passover festival, many believed in his name, for they could see the signs he was performing. For his part, Jesus would not trust himself to them because he knew them all.
>
> John 2:23–24

What Jesus knew was that Temple cleansers and wine multipliers (the two preceding incidents are the wedding feast of Cana and the cleansing of the Temple) attract crowds. Sign-makers draw sign-watchers. Nothing more, nothing less.

This canniness of Christ, his shrewd ability to inhabit the interior of people, is the fine irony at the center of the episode at the house of Simon the Pharisee. Simon thinks to himself that Jesus is not a prophet because he does not know that the woman who touches him is a sinner. The next line is "In answer to his [Simon's] thoughts . . . " (Lk. 7:40). Jesus may not be enough of a prophet to know what type of woman it is who touches him, but he is enough of a prophet to know what

Simon is thinking. Jesus has the ability to move inside the people he is dealing with even as they think he lacks this ability.

Other gospel stories also stress this heart-reading ability. In the story of the cure of the paralytic (Mk. 2:8; Lk. 5:22), Jesus is aware of the reasoning of the Pharisees, "though they kept it to themselves." He knows the thoughts of the Pharisees who come to spy on him in order that they might find something to charge him with (Lk. 6:8). He discerns the thoughts of the disciples as they argue among themselves over who will be the greatest (Lk. 9:47). He knows his disciples murmur against his sayings (Jn. 6:61). In one of the resurrection narratives (Lk. 24:38), he says, even though the disciples had not spoken, "Why do such ideas cross your mind?"

What are we to make of this heart-reading ability? We can take this in a magical way, that he possessed some extraordinary power which permitted him to eavesdrop on the interior conversations of his friends and adversaries. Or when we stress that Jesus is the God-Man, we can attribute this to his divine knowledge which knows all things and bypasses the normal modes of communication. But there is another possibility, a possibility that avoids magical leaps and allows Jesus' unique relationship to God and the knowledge that gives him to be mediated through attentive human perceptions.

The heart is never directly on display. It is well hidden, and in order to read it, some detective work is needed. What is observable is people talking and acting. What is observable is the hidden spiritual center, the assumptions about God and neighbor, which are prompting the words and actions. "Each man [woman] speaks from his [her] heart's abundance" (Lk. 6:45). The genius of Jesus the Master is that he sees the connection between the abundance of the heart and the speech. He attends to the proximate in order to discern the ultimate, the fundamental attitudes toward God and neighbor.

We have explored this way of knowing—from the seen to the unseen—when we detailed the dynamics of fascination and when we approached the life and death of Jesus. It is also the key to appreciating how Jesus responds to people. He often avoids the surface comments and actions and directs himself to the depth of the person which is revealed in the surface comments and action. He discerns where the person is "coming from" and it is that reality that he wishes to address.

> Someone in the crowd said to him, "Teacher, tell my brother to give me my share of our inheritance." He replied, "Friend, who has set me up as your judge or arbiter?"
>
> Luke 12:13–14

The man wants a decision. Instead, Jesus uncovers the assumptive world of his request. Jesus sees him as someone who is using him to get what he wants. He has no qualms about breaking the relationship with his brother for the sake of the inheritance. He will be a divider, and he wants Jesus to command the division. It is this heart which underlies the request, and it is this heart that Jesus unmasks and challenges.

> As they were making their way along, someone said to him, "I will be your follower wherever you go." Jesus said to him, "The foxes have lairs, the birds of the sky have nests, but the Son of Man has nowhere to lay his head"
>
> Luke 9:57–58

In this simple remark, Jesus hears a boast that knows nothing of hardship. More importantly, he hears a confidence of conviction which does not acknowledge that perseverance is the gift of God. Jesus addresses himself to this interior exuberance, not to negate it, but to sober it. The words of the man reveal his personal center. The personal center needs some correction.

The enigmatic words of Jesus to Pilate in the trial scene of Mark suggest the same type of interchange: "Pilate interrogated him: 'Are you the king of the Jews?' 'You are the one who is saying it,' Jesus replied" (Mk. 15:2). Is Jesus at the hidden center of Pilate which knows the truth of the title King of the Jews? Is the one accused judging the judge? The picture of Pilate in Mark might lead one in that direction. He asks other questions of Jesus in an attempt to help him, and he tries to release Jesus. But the crowds chose Barabbas, and he gives in to their demands. But even here, Jesus is acting as the Master and attempting to uncover the heart of the procurator.

This capacity of Jesus to read the heart, to see in the immediate the manifestations of the ultimate, came from the unity of his own person. Jesus himself lived out of his personal relationship to God, a relationship which grounded and influenced his relationship to all other things. This interior relationship manifested itself in his attitudes, thoughts, and actions. What people heard and saw was what he was. His inner unity with God was evident n his outer unity with people. There was a transparency about him, an integration, a wholism.

Ben Meyer has some insightful remarks in his summation of the life of Jesus:

> . . . we are better positioned to grasp the transparence and coherence of Jesus' career: his proclamation, his teaching, his choice and sending of the twelve, his exorcisms and cures, his table fellowship with the outcast, his demonstration at the temple, his distribution of loaf and cup at the Last

> Supper. It was difficult to bring into uniform focus the range of meaning carried by all these words and actions; but in itself every word, every act, was mountain water . . . Though his actions and the purposes that informed them were of themselves entirely out of the ordinary, they were none the less diaphanous.[5]

The radiance of the hidden spiritual center of Jesus illumines every word and deed. There is an unbroken harmony between who he is and what he does. This unity of the person of Jesus is attested to on almost every page of the Gospels and writ large in the Church's tradition by the great doctrine of the hypostatic union.

What Jesus was in himself, he discerned in others. Since he was a person whose fundamental relationship to God and neighbor suffused all he did and said, he sensed that connection in others. And he placed great importance on it:

> "Do you ever pick grapes from thornbushes, or figs from prickly plants? Never! . . . A sound tree cannot bear bad fruit any more than a decayed tree can bear good fruit"
>
> Matthew 7:16, 18

The tree is the fundamental relationship to God and neighbor. Our words and actions correspond to the fruit. The same observation is made by contrast in the following sequence:

> "It is not what goes into a man's mouth that makes him impure; it is what comes out of his mouth . . . Do you not see that everything that enters the mouth passes into the stomach and is discharged

> into the latrine, but what comes out of the mouth
> originates in the mind?
>
> Matthew 15:11,17–18a

Jesus senses in people what he knows in himself—a hidden spiritual center that energizes thought, feeling, and action.

These reflections provide our first clue to gain entry into some of the gospel stories. We will focus on the personal interaction of Jesus with people, and we will try to understand the posture of their heart, their ultimate orientation to God and neighbor. We will be able to uncover this heart if we attend to their observable words and actions and the rare direct clues the gospel writer might provide. But more importantly, if we attend to what Jesus says to them and ask why he says that, we will begin to see what the Master sees. That, after all, is what the disciple wants.

Techniques

Many of Jesus' speeches in the Gospels appear to be rambling, patchwork monologues. But since the Gospels are narratives—people interacting with people which develops a plot—our assumption is that he is always talking to someone. He addresses the crowds, his disciples, the priests, the Pharisees, and individuals. Jesus also talks to God, and in one scene, God talks to him (Lk. 3:22). But at those times, we realize that Jesus, the Master, is himself a disciple. The Father is apprenticing his Son in the ways of the Kingdom.

All these people whom Jesus talks to are in a particular place; their fundamental relationship to God and neighbor is construed in a certain way. Jesus' efforts will be geared to get them to see things as he does. In order to do this, he employs various techniques, strategies to help the people contact the reality he knows. *Technique* and *strategy* are words that can smack of manipulation. They seem to imply a self-conscious superiority, an overly thought-out plan of attack.

But Jesus' techniques and strategies are integrated into his role as Master. They are elements in his art of loving. His total project is to apprentice the person into a relationship with Abba, his Father. Whatever will make that happen, Jesus is willing to dare. The ultimate refutation that Jesus' techniques and strategies are manipulative ways to maintain his own power is that his final "technique and strategy" to bring people into the love of God was to die.

It is helpful to have some knowledge of Jesus' art. Our final goal is to be his faithful disciple. If we understand how he relates, we may be more receptive to his words and actions. But we must respect the fact that we cannot reduce his volatile personal style to a series of moves. He is so subtle and responsive a presence that the only thing that is truly predictable is that he will be unpredictable. But we should appreciate the way the Master questions; praises; confronts; and, through storytelling, transposes people into different yet similar worlds. These will be some of the techniques he will use as he trains us in his way of life.

Jesus is a man of many questions. Sometimes they are rhetorical: "How can the guests at a wedding fast as long as the groom is still among them?" (Mk. 2:19). "Is a lamp acquired to be put under a bushel basket or hidden under a bed? Is it not meant to be put on a stand?" (Mk. 4:21). "Or if a king is about to march on another king to do battle with him, will he not sit down first and consider whether, with ten thousand men, he can withstand an enemy coming against him with twenty thousand?" (Lk. 14:31).

Sometimes these questions are probing: "Why do you make this din with your wailing?" (Mk. 5:39). "What do you want me to do for you?" (Lk. 18:41). "Do you think that these

Galileans were the greatest sinners in Galilee just because they suffered this?" (Lk. 13:2). The Master knows who to ask what and when to ask it, and he does not back off easily.

But the actual import of any question cannot be decided in the abstract. The context governs its significance. The probing question "What do you suppose the owner of the vineyard will do to those tenants when he comes?" (Mt. 21:40), is really a solicitation of self-judgment from his listeners. And the double rhetorical question "Who, in fact, is the greater—he who reclines at table or he who serves the meal? Is it not the one who reclines at table?" is really a set-up for the next line—"Yet I am in your midst as the one who serves you" (Lk. 22:27). Jesus' questions are aimed at specific people and groups, and to understand their intent, we must discern their spiritual state.

Whether the questions are rhetorical or probative and whatever their context is, they are meant to be answered. Silence is the way of avoidance and the most effective way to break down the learning relationship. In the famous scene where Peter confesses Jesus as the Son of the Living God, he is commended for his correct answer which came from God (Mt. 16:13–20). But he is also commended just because he answered.

"Who do you say that I am?" was a question to all. Peter risked the interaction, and Jesus rewarded him with an introduction into the strange allegiance of divine and human revelation ("No mere man has revealed this to you, but my heavenly Father") and into the peculiar character of his own mission ("You are 'Rock,' and on this rock . . . ").

We stressed that Jesus was a master who engaged his disciples. Monologues are for monomaniacs. Jesus liked revelatory exchanges with words which "penetrate and divides soul and spirit, joints and marrow; it judges the reflections and thoughts of the heart" (Heb. 4:12). Questioning did this. It was Jesus' way of drawing people close, of engaging them, of making the Kingdom near at hand.

Another strategy of Jesus was commendation. When Jesus encountered attitudes and actions which reflected life in the Kingdom, he praised them. A centurion is praised because he knows the secret of the chain of command (Lk. 7:1–10). A scribe is told he is not far from the Kingdom of God because he is one step removed from the altar of sacrifice (Mk. 12:28–34). A persistent, crying woman is reluctantly lauded because she undoes Jesus' ethnicity (Mt. 15:21–28). A widow without surplus gives from her want, and Jesus cheers (Mk. 12:41–44). A leper comes back in gratitude and Jesus declares him saved while nine others are only healed (Lk. 17:11–19). A woman with a jar of perfume does not use it on herself and is told that she and the good news will be inseparable (Mk. 14:3–9). Children who have accumulated nothing are put forth as examples of inheriting the Kingdom (Mk. 10:13–16). Also blessed are the poor, the sorrowing, the hungering, the thirsting, the merciful, the peacemakers, and the persecuted (Mt. 5:3–12). Jesus is a master of affirmation.

As an element in the master-disciple relationship praise means progress. The person is walking in the way of Jesus and beginning to be human as Jesus is human. But this way of being human which Jesus proposes is not valued in the society as a whole. The society gives few rewards to the people Jesus praises and few accolades to the attitudes he prizes. So the Master himself makes up for this oversight. He and his Father are the support system for his radical way of life to such an extent that he is everywhere present to it.

As the disciples continue his way of compassion and service, they will meet him in the least of the brothers and sisters and he will honor them, "Come. You have my Father's blessing!" (Mt. 25:34). This supportive praise of Jesus is always genuine. The sincerity of Jesus' approval can be gauged by the reverse tactic of noting the sincerity of his disapproval. As the poet has suggested, Jesus' "Yes" was forged in the smithy of a 1,000 noes.

Confrontation was also a continual factor in Jesus' relationships. It was necessary because people's words and deeds betrayed hearts of stone. In other words, their hearts were wrongly positioned in relationship to God and neighbor, and this had to be called to their attention. Sometimes the confrontation was mild, a mere correction. When a woman praises Mary because she is his biological mother, Jesus corrects her: "Rather . . . blest are they who hear the word of God and keep it" (Lk. 11:28). When the disciples try to keep the children from him, Jesus is irritated and says, "Let the children come to me" (Mk. 10:14). The Master is pointing out a more perfect perception of his mother and a more welcoming attitude toward children.

But there was also more strenuous confrontation. J. K. Kadowaki, working out of the Zen tradition, specifies spiritual confrontation as "stopping the flow of delusion."[6] People are thinking and feeling along a certain trajectory, but this line of thought and feeling is delusory and should not be indulged. No matter what the exact words of direct confrontation are, the message is "Stop it!"

The classic instance of this strategy is Jesus' forceful response to Peter's horror and subsequent prayer that Jesus might not suffer (Mt. 16:21–23). He calls Peter "Satan" and tells him to "get behind me." In other words, he must return to the role of a disciple and follow behind Jesus, to allow Jesus to teach him the way of the Kingdom. Peter has let his thinking stray down the path of the human, fearful, anxious thoughts of success and glory. Jesus' strong words attempt to stem this "flow of delusion" and bring Peter back to the way of the Kingdom.

That is not the only time that Jesus sternly confronts Peter. At the Last Supper (Lk. 22:31–34), Jesus has just finished praying for Peter and has subtly indicated that his faith will be shaken, but "when he turns," he will strengthen his brothers and sisters. Jesus perceives Peter as vulnerable to temptation but with great power to recover and start again. Peter responds, "Lord, . . . at your side I am prepared to face imprisonment and death itself."

Peter perceives himself as steadfast and unyielding. He has taken his nickname of "Rock" to heart. Jesus replies, "I tell you, Peter, the cock will not crow today until you have three times denied that you know me." Once again, Peter is caught in a delusory flow of thought, only this time it is not about Jesus' destiny but about his own character. Peter does not know himself, nor does he rely on prayer and divine help in the midst of trial. He boldly states his own virtue. Jesus' tactic is a direct attack which hopefully will force Peter to reappraise himself.

This type of strong confrontation tries to unmask hidden assumptions and dislodge deeply entrenched attitudes and perceptions. There is nothing gentle about it. The affirming Jesus is gone. A head-to-head, no-blinking person has taken his place. When the Sadducees rehearse their afterlife fiasco of one wife and seven brothers, Jesus' return volley is "You are badly misled, because you fail to understand the Scriptures or the power of God" (Mk. 12:24).

After Jesus blasts the Pharisees, a lawyer says, "Teacher, in speaking this way you insult us too." Jesus not only does not honor his complaint but puts him in the same category as the Pharisees, "Woe to you lawyers also!" (Lk. 11:45–46). When James and John ask to sit at the right and left of Jesus, he says straightforwardly, "You do not know what you are asking" (Mk. 10:38). All these interactions show a master who refuses to be compromised by the distorted perceptions and attitudes of the people he encounters.

Jesus' language plays a major role in the way he confronts. He uses forceful and imaginative language which has tremendous shock value and uncovers in flashes, like lightening illumining the sky, the darkened areas of our heart.[7] "When you give alms . . . do not blow a horn . . . " confronts our deep need to win approval from others (Mt. 6:1–2). "When a person strikes you on the right cheek, turn and offer him the other . . . " challenges our natural instinct for revenge (Mt. 5:39). "Consider the ravens . . . " addresses our drive to hoard and pretend we have transcended the limits of finite life (Lk. 12:24). The images of trumpets, slaps, and birds have a special power to make us stop and consider.

Part of this special power of imaginative language, especially when it contains shocking contrasts, is that it can provoke insight. Sharp, forceful language and realized understanding are partners. Our normal structures of perception are impervious to debate and hours of tedious argument. But often they can be shattered by a single blow. If the right words are said at the right time, the scales may fall from our eyes. Some of the right words which the Master spoke were:

> "No man can serve two masters" (Mt. 6:24); "Who aspires to greatness must serve the rest" (Mk. 10:43); "Whoever will save his life will lose it, and whoever loses his life for my sake will save it" (Lk. 9:24); "Let the dead bury their dead" (Lk. 9:60); "Whoever puts his hand to the plow but keeps looking back is unfit for the reign of God" (Lk. 9:62); "Even the hairs of your head are counted!" (Lk. 12:7);

> "The gift you have received, give as a gift" (Mt. 10:8); "The sabbath was made for man, not man for the sabbath" (Mk. 2:27); "Is not life more than food?" (Mt. 6:25); "To those who have, more will be given; from those who have not, what little they have will be taken away" (Mk. 4:25). "It is easier for a camel to pass through a needle's eye than for a rich man to enter the kingdom of God" (Mt. 19:24).

What these one-liners evoke may be spelled out in conceptual discourse, but the instantaneous dismantling and remantling of perception that they can trigger and the delight of the Master when that happened earned Jesus an image: "A sharp, two-edged sword came out of his mouth, and his face shone like the sun at its brightest" (Rev. 1:16).

J. K. Kadowaki gives both a funny and an illuminating example of the effect of imaginative and forceful language. "A monk inquired earnestly of Unmon, 'What is Buddha?' Unmon said, 'A dried shit stick.'" Kadowaki goes on to explain what Unmon, the master, is trying to achieve.

> If, instead of replying directly, Unmon had explained, "All being is kept in existence by the life of Buddha; therefore, a dried shit stick is endowed with the Buddha and it goes without saying that your body is too," the questioner may have apprehended it intellectually and felt he understood but it would never have become a wisdom that he could vigorously put to practical use in everyday life . . . It is not enough to know this conceptually; you must experience it with your "body." This kind of realization is called an unthought thought, impossible to express no matter how exhaustively you explain it.[8]

Imaginative language can "tear down and build up" with one well-placed phrase. Its concrete character facilitates insight which brings about a new way of seeing and which the creative disciples can translate into action. When the imaginative language of Jesus has this type of impact, the Master and the disciple are moving toward friendship.

Another technique of Jesus is transposition. He accomplishes this through storytelling. After he has discerned the hearts of the people, he will often tell them a story which will allow them both a distance from and an intimacy with their lives. The story transposes them into its world and urges them to feel its problems and possibilities as their own.

The listeners see things in the story they cannot see in their own lives, and they are free to evaluate people in the story in a way that they are not free to do in their actual situations. But the story, in its fundamental structure, is remarkably like the situation in which they live. When they return to their actual world, they see it differently: they see it through the new eyes the story has given them. From their actual world to the story world and back to their actual world is the transposition which the art of the Master makes possible.

This understanding of transposition is rooted in the "natural" processes of interpretation. In fact, there is something in the nature of stories in general and of Jesus' stories in particular that demands participation by the listener.

> The parables invite, even compel the interpreter to become a creator, to engage the text by joining in the creation of its meaning. In so doing he or she not only opens the parable story to current issues and problems but also opens himself or herself to the process of understanding the story. The context and the focus chosen by the interpreter spring from

> the personal system of meaning embraced by that particular human being. Thus the process of interpreting the parables can reveal much about the values, concerns, and priorities of the individual.[9]

The Master wants people to enter the story with their "personal system of meaning" and to return to their actual lives with those "personal systems of meaning" transformed.

In the gospel, we are often given clues to the meaning-system of the people who listen to Jesus' stories. Sometimes the designation is vague. Jesus told the story of the corrupt judge to people who pray. "He told them a parable on the necessity of praying always and not losing heart" (Lk. 18:1). The parable of the Pharisee and the tax collector is told to those "who believed in their own self-righteousness, while holding everyone else in contempt" (Lk. 18:9). The story of the returning king who interrogates his servants is told to those who "thought that the reign of God was about to appear" (Lk. 19:11). The parables of the lost coin, the lost sheep, and lost son are addressed to Pharisees and scribes who murmured, "This man welcomes sinners and eats with them" (Lk. 15:1–2). When we know who Jesus is talking to, we can better understand his intentions and his choice of stories.

At other times, the parables are addressed to individuals or to more clearly defined groups. The story of the two debtors is told to Simon (Lk. 7:36–50); the story of the good Samaritan is told to the lawyer (Lk. 10:25–37); the story of the two sons is told to the chief priest and elders (Mt. 21:28–31); the story of the rich fool is triggered by a young man who wants his inheritance (Lk. 12:13–21); the story of the great supper is told to the Pharisees at a banquet (Lk. 14:12–24); the stories of the sower and the seed, the seed growing secretly, the mustard seed (Mk. 4:1–32), and the vineyard workers (Mt. 20:1–16) are told to the disciples. All these people are asked to enter the story as they are and return with whatever they have found.

But the stories of Jesus as part of the Master's repertoire can be considered in two other contexts. Contemporary scholarship has often tried to deconstruct the actual gospel settings of the parables and reconstruct the first listeners. A prime example of this is the good Samaritan (Lk. 10:30–35). It is taken out of its Lukan context where the hearer of the story is a lawyer bent on self-justification and placed in a setting where the hearers would be Samaritan-hating Jews. This story is now interacting with different systems of personal meanings and therefore triggering different spiritual movements.

For many people, retrieving the historical situation of Jesus is a much-needed touchstone. When we understand the original impact of his person and message, we have a way of evaluating later developments. The spiritual transpositions the stories encouraged at the beginning should not be lost.

A third context of the stories is paradoxically the story itself. The stories can be appropriated strictly in terms of their internal dynamics. They stand as stories with ordinary yet unusual characters and familiar yet strange plots. The personal systems of meaning belong to the characters themselves, and it is their spiritual movements which are highlighted. When we approach the stories in this way, they are free from their confining contexts in the Gospels and in the world of Jesus' mission and ministry and open to some very intriguing interpretations. Earl Breech synopsizes the story of the great feast:

> Jesus tells the story of the congenial man who wanted to give a great feast (Luke 14:16–24 and par.) and who, because he was enraged that his invited guests had things to do which prevented

> them from coming on time or prevented them from coming at all, ended up, because of his irascibility, eating with strangers brought in from the streets and the country. Here, a man's anger isolates him from others, in spite of his original intentions.[10]

The transposition happens to the people within the story and the listener, in whatever culture or age of history, identifies with those characters and undergoes similar dynamics. As Breech interprets that story, the reader is drawn into the world of self-isolating anger. The Master is helping the disciple understand that loneliness can result out of the invitation to party.

No matter what contexts and personal systems of meaning are involved—the people in the Gospels, the original audience of Jesus, or the people within the stories—it is important to understand the role of the Master's stories. It is often ballyhooed that Jesus is a storyteller. It is as if this act in itself said it all. But it does not say half enough. His purpose in telling stories is not to entertain or even to portray the human condition in its rich variety of glory and folly. His purpose is to transport people into another world so that they can return to see and act in their own world in a new way.

The question is not whether Jesus told great stories; he certainly did that. The question is whether we allow the stories to instruct our spirit. If we do, the storyteller becomes the Master.

Third-Party Discipleship

Third-party discipleship begins with an imaginative entry into the scriptural stories of Jesus' encounters with people. We listen closely to the words of both the people and the Master; we watch closely the actions of both the people and the Master. We ask why Jesus asked that question and why the people answered in the way they did. We ask why Jesus praised that person and confronted that person. We ask how the story Jesus told would be heard by those people. What would it affirm and what would it shatter in them? As we watch Jesus act as a master to the people in the Gospels, he becomes a master for us. We are third-party disciples.

At the beginning of this chapter, we stressed that once we enter the text, we must be patient and receptive. Prayer is a correct word for this form of participation. But we must also be knowledgeable. The more we know about the literary form of the story and the historical situations which it reflects, the more we will be attuned to what the Master is doing. In the life of a disciple, prayer and study are complementary activities.

What might happen to us as third-party disciples? Two distinct yet connected scenarios seem to happen over and over again. They are occasioned by two ways of being in the story. Sometimes a highly personal encounter with Jesus mediated through the story occurs. The exchange in the story between Jesus and the people quickly becomes an exchange between Jesus and us. We are opened up by his questions, praised and confronted, and if he tells us a story, it is a mirror of truth. Jesus looks at us, directly and unflinchingly.

At these times we are not in a "removed" place saying, "Well, that is an interesting insight; I wonder what it means for me?" There is no need for translation. What Jesus teaches us and what we must do with the teaching are immediately evident. If a hermeneutic process is at work, it is not a laborious plodding from the world of the text to our world. The two worlds instantly fuse, and we are weighed in the balance.

At other times, we are "in" the story but not "of" the story. Immediacy and involvement do not characterize our participation. We gather wisdom, note the patterns of judgment, understand some of the dynamics of sin and redemption. But the lightening application of the first way of being in the story does not happen. We are obviously in two worlds which do not easily fuse, and we must move from one to the other via analogies.

We have to discern the fundamental attitudes toward God and neighbor which are present in those first-century issues—Sabbath observance, ritual washings, the place of the Temple, dietary customs, exorcisms, and so on. Then we must find similar attitudes among ourselves as we argue over twentieth-century issues. What we must discern and correlate are the basic human attitudes that are manifest as the gospel people argue their issues and as we argue our issues. This is the transcultural dimension of the human spirit which is the real interest of the Spirit Master.

What are the results of being in the story in either an immediate or a removed way? The premier response is action. In action, insight is made concrete and discipleship becomes real. In action, whatever fears we have must be confronted and overcome. Moments of new perception are just that—moments. The recognition of the liberating possibility of a new attitude is just that—recognition.

In the third-party encounter with Jesus, the door that suddenly opens may just as suddenly shut. The way to put your foot in the door, to be actually changed by the perception or attitude which is received, is to act on it. In this way, the learning which flows from the third-party encounter is stabilized and made permanent. Once this advance in the way of Jesus is a reality, a habit of mind, heart, and feet, then the Master moves again, and discipleship moves toward friendship.

But there are other responses besides action. We can express in language what we received from our training with Jesus. We can articulate the wisdom of his way. And this secondary, but important, response will be the way we will proceed. This is a book, a feast of print, written by a person who eats words and presumably read by people who eat words. So we will put some more words on the table.

We have looked at the art of the Master, but we have not explored that art in action. We have not watched the Master at work, and so in the next chapter we will observe Jesus as he apprentices people into the way of being human he calls the Kingdom of God. If we meet the reality of God which he lives "in and out of," we will begin to call the Master "friend." Friendship means we are "living in and out of" the reality he "lives in and out of." Therefore, the final section will be to tell stories about that reality which the gospel stories engender, to make contemporary the way of Jesus in brief narratives. It is not the premier response of a disciple, but it is not silence either.

CHAPTER SIX

The Master at Work

The Lord will give you the bread you need
and the water for which you thirst.
No longer will your Teacher hide himself,
but with your own eyes you shall see your Teacher,
While from behind, a voice shall sound in your ears:
"This is the way; walk in it."

Isaiah 30:20–21

The Lord GOD has given me
a well-trained tongue,
That I might know how to speak to the weary
a word that will rouse them.

Isaiah 50:4

Jesus is the teacher who does not hide himself. Jesus speaks to many different types in the Gospels—religious leaders, the crowds, anonymous speakers shouting questions or comments from the crowd, the petitioning sick and possessed, countless individuals who come for advice or a favor. Jesus works with them all. He applies his art on whomever he meets to bring them a little closer to the reality of God and neighbor he sees so clearly. Yet with his disciples he seems to take special care. They will be the foremost people who will carry on his mission and way of life, and so with them he works assiduously. They bring him his greatest joy ("I have greatly desired to eat this Passover with you" Lk. 22:14) and some of his most recurring irritations ("How long can I endure you?" Lk. 9:41).

Therefore, we will try to move within and participate in three of Jesus' training sessions with his disciples. We will try to pay attention to Jesus' "well-trained tongue that can rouse the weary." We will see if he can talk to us while he is talking to them. We might come out of these sessions slightly shocked, seeing things a little differently than we did before. There may be some perceptual shift. Or we may emerge with some wisdom about the perennial human condition which, at the moment, we do not know how to apply. This wisdom is not lost, but stored, and it has a way of surfacing in our lives when we least want it but most need it. If we would be a disciple, we must submit to the Master.

We will briefly enter into two of Jesus's instructions and try to follow the thoughts and feelings he is trying to evoke in his disciples. In the first session, his disciples are riding high on success and joy (Lk. 10:17–20). The Master takes this joy, relates it to God, and returns it to them. In the second session they are bent low with fear (Lk. 12:4–7). The Master takes this fear and relates it to God, but unlike their joy, he refuses to return their fear back to them.

In a final and longer exploration, we will watch Jesus fail as he attempts to teach a young man how to relate to the goodness of God. Then where he failed with the young man, the Master will try to succeed with his disciples. He will strive with all his art to communicate to them the intricacies of his way of life which is based on the goodness of God. At the end, we will not know whether he has succeeded with his disciples (Mt. 19:16—20:16). But we will have to answer whether he has succcceded with us.

Luke 10:17–20

> The seventy-two returned in jubilation saying, "Master, even the demons are subject to us in your name."

The disciples are returning from being out on their own. They had reached a point where they knew enough of the way of Jesus and were familiar enough with the power of God to pass it on. They were extensions of Jesus' mission. Their success made them happy. Enough of the power of God was working through them to chase demons. But I see them—in the light of what Jesus is about to say—as mindlessly enthusiastic over their new-found powers.

"Master, even the demons are subject to us" is a giddy shout. Then an embarrassed silence as they realize whom they are talking to. This is the one they call "Master," the one who has trained them and had more confidence in them than they had in themselves. They quickly add, "in your name." Jesus, the Master, notices the pause:

> He said in reply: "I watched Satan fall from the sky like lightning."

Jesus confirms their success and joins in their joy. In fact, he attempts to escalate their happiness. They have rousted a few demons; Jesus sees the end of Satan's reign. Jesus' confidence in them is unbounded, his affirmation wildly hyperbolic. Picture yourself coming home from wherever you toil. "How was your day?" asks the one you come home to. "I did some good things," you reply. "I know," says the one you tell. "While you were out there doing good things, I saw Satan fall from the sky like lightning." I would call that support.

> "See what I have done; I have given you power to tread on snakes and scorpions and all the forces of the enemy, and nothing shall ever injure you."

Jesus continues his affirmation of their growing powers and underlines the fact that they are greater than the forces of destruction. But with a twist. He relates what they have done to him. He is the one who gave them the power to do it. He picks up and corrects the pause between "demons subject to us" and "in your name." He has moved their joy, gently but definitely, from glorying in what they had done to a sense of indebtedness to him for giving them the power. The Jesus who accepts our concerns also transforms them. But he is not done yet. (In the next encounter we will consider—Lk. 12:4–7—we will be treated to what Jesus considers injury and why his disciples are beyond it.)

> "Nevertheless, do not rejoice so much in the fact that devils are subject to you as that your names are inscribed in heaven."

Watch out when Jesus uses *nevertheless.* Some transforming perception is about to be communicated. First, he gives them back what he momentarily took away. He took their power and tied it to his own so they would know it was not theirs alone. Now he says what they said: "devils are subject to you," and that is a cause for rejoicing. But the reason for the rejoicing is not that you have power, but that through you the ultimate power has effected its purpose. Their power was in Jesus' name, but Jesus' power is in God's name. "Hallowed be your name" (Lk. 11:2). That their names are inscribed in heaven means that the power of God has been glorified and that they have been part of it. Their names, Jesus' name, and God's name are written together.

The Master began with where they were—happy with their success. He affirmed their success with a lavishness greater than they presented it. He tied their new-found powers to his own apprenticing of them. In this way, he added gratitude to joy. And finally, he tied gratitude and joy to the power of God which relativizes the ego and increases the sense of mission.

He led them to the source and in the process transformed their initial jubilation, not into sadness, but into gratitude and hope.

How Jesus sees it takes nothing away from what happened and who accomplished it. It just adds and adds and adds. The master takes them, fresh from a skirmish on earth and leads them into heaven, a heaven that Satan has recently fallen from, where they see what he sees—his Father writing their names in the Book of Life.

Luke 12:4–7

> "I say to you who are my friends:"

Jesus is talking to his friends, but they are in a "crowd of thousands . . . so dense that they were treading on one another." Perhaps if they can overhear what Jesus is saying to his friends, they too will become his friends. We already know how friendship with Jesus develops and so we can guess where this conversation is going.

> "Do not be afraid of those who kill the body and can do no more."

This advice of Jesus is wonderful but impossible to achieve. We fear what can kill the body. Much of our outer life is taken up with avoiding those situations and people who will do us bodily harm. Our inner life worries about aging, fears pain, and escalates a sore throat into cancer. To be part of the embodied human race is to fear being disembodied.

> Therefore, if Jesus is serious about being able to live without fear of bodily destruction, he must supply us with the necessary resources. To command lack of fear is merely to increase guilt. Before Jesus spoke we were afraid, but we thought it was

> normal, that it came with the territory of finitude. Now we are told it is possible not to be afraid of what can kill the body. But of course, we continue to fear, only now because we are not supposed to, we add guilt to fear and our present state is worse than our first. Thanks to Jesus. He has put us in a peculiar predicament, and the last line of his advice seems to say there is more to come: "and can do no more."

> "I will show you whom you ought to fear."

At this stage, Jesus is not trying to eliminate fear but attempting to focus it properly. He is speaking in the first person and, therefore, throwing the full weight of his authority behind his words.

> "Fear him who has power to cast into Gehenna after he has killed."

This is hardly consolation. Fear has been escalated from physical harm into everlasting loss. For one who knows Gehenna, the ever-burning garbage dump outside of Jerusalem, the new fear is more horrible than the old one. An analogy, which stays on the physical level, might be the story about a man who falls off a curb. His ankle is in pain. "I fear I broke my ankle," the man tells his doctor. "Don't worry about it," the doctor says. "When we discover the bone cancer, that fear will go away." Jesus is that doctor.

> "Yes, I tell you, fear him."

Jesus commands fear. It now appears that his previous injunction was not against fear but against misplaced fear. He has now named the ultimate reality which has power to cause thc ultimate injury. Anyone who is even mildly allergic to logic must see that this is the reality to cringe before. Jesus' strategy is to get fear out in the open. Fear flourishes when it is concealed. When it is hidden and its proper object is not focused, it exercises tremendous influence in our lives.

> "Are not five sparrows sold for a few pennies? Yet not one of them is neglected by God."

By direct commands, Jesus has brought the disciples into heightened consciousness of fear. Command language is appropriate to fear. Now he will transform the fear by image and suggestion. He begins by underlining the insignificant market value of sparrows. Yet despite this, God, the one who has the power to cast into Gehenna, is concerned with each.

> "In very truth, even the hairs of your head are counted!"

This is the "very truth" that Jesus wants to "slam home." What we ultimately fear knows us and cares for us more than we know and care for ourselves. God sweeps the floor of the barber shop.

> "Fear nothing, then."

The conclusion comes in the form of a counter command. From "fear him" to "fear nothing" is the path of the liberation of the spirit. This passage charts the path of love which is outlined in 1 Jn. 4:18:

> Love has no room for fear;
> rather perfect love casts out all fear.
> And since fear has to do with punishment,
> love is not yet perfect in one who is afraid.

It is necessary for the deepest fears of the human heart to be exposed if they are to be healed. As long as a thousand little fears snap like dogs at our heels, we will not face the deepest fear which Cyril of Jerusalem called the dragon that sits by the side of the road: the fear that even if we are healthy, wealthy, and wise, we are ultimately waste, destined for the garbage heap outside Jerusalem called Gehenna.

"You are worth more than a flock of sparrows."

It is difficult to articulate the overwhelming affection of this understatement. This is a line of love that takes an image of human insignificance and turns it into a playful assurance of human worth. We might get an inkling of this way of playful assurance if we "fool" with another one of Jesus' images.

The man sighs, "Look at these flowers in the field. Here today and gone tomorrow. No trace. Just like us."

The woman says, "I would personally say that you are like a mixed bouquet. When you have a vodka gimlet, your lips purse up like a tulip. You sit on a couch like a sprawled chrysanthemum. After a day on the beach, you look like a daisy in August. You laugh like a lily and cry like a daffodil. I would say you are worth a whole hothouse of flowers."

If we enter into this passage with our full affective life and move through its dynamics, we should end in laughter. This is the laughter Conrad Hyers calls "the laughter of paradise regained."[1] It is the laughter that has undergone evil and found itself, if only momentarily, in a place of profound affirmation.

This laughter comes from a "sense of security rather than insecurity . . . It presupposes faith in some sacred order or depth-dimension of being, some common basis of worth and dignity."[2]

It is my suspicion that this laughter of salvation can only go on among friends who share, not a secret, but good news.

Jesus began this instruction on fear by calling his disciples "friends" because he was going to tell them something he had heard from someone else. The Gospel of John knows who that someone else is. "I call you friends, since I have made known to you all that I heard from my Father" (Jn. 15:15).

Matthew 19:16–20:16

> Another time a man came up to him and said, "Teacher, what good must I do to possess everlasting life?"

The man addresses Jesus as teacher, and he is about to taught. But if our prejudices about acceptance, transformation, and hope are correct, what he will learn is not exactly what he has in mind. His request sounds normal enough. In fact, it is a request that most catechists would love to hear. It signals interest. Someone wants to know about everlasting life. But Jesus hears more in the request than sincere interest.

> He answered, "Why do you question me about what is good? There is One who is good. If you wish to enter into life, keep the commandments."

Jesus returns a question with a question. He wants to know the "why" of it all. What is the spiritual state that generates this type of question? Jesus senses a distorted understanding of the relationship to God. This distortion centers around the words *good* and *possess.* Jesus leaps on the word *good*. He may want to know why the man is asking him about the good and not God, the One who is good.

But more probably, Jesus wants to know why the man has (1) connected goodness with himself and (2) considers his own goodness capable of bringing him everlasting life. God alone is good, and it is out of the goodness of God that everlasting life is made available. This man's initial request is being drastically amended. The focus is no longer on himself but on God.

With this correction, Jesus returns to his request, but changes the wording from "possess" to "enter into." Everlasting life is not an object to be possessed but a Mystery of indwelling and enjoyment. It is not something we own but a Reality we can participate in. The way to participate in it is to embrace the way of life the "One who is good" has given. Living in line with the commandments means communicating with the living out the power of everlasting life.

> "Which ones?" he asked.
>
> Jesus replied: "'You shall not kill'; 'You shall not commit adultery'; 'You shall not steal'; 'You shall not bear false witness'; 'Honor your father and mother'; and 'Love your neighbor as yourself.'"
>
> The young man said to him, "I have kept all these; what do I need to do further?"

This man has not heard Jesus' correction of his request. All he has heard is the linking of "commandments" to his initial aggressive, ego-centered attitude. Now he knows the good he must do. But much like an anxious student who demands to know "which questions" will be on the test, this young man must know precisely what will get him what he wants. The inner drive to possess always wants to make sure. His question "Which ones?" reflects this anxious, acquisitive spirit. This second question is on the same track as the first question, and his first question was wrongheaded.

Jesus' response attempts to address him on two levels. On one level, Jesus is trying to calm the agitation of "Which ones?"

He patiently recites the commandments that make for life, soothing the troubled spirit, stroking the anxiety. The Master does not break the bruised reed or quench the smoldering wick (Mt. 12:20). A Buddhist story may illumine this process and also prepare for what is to come:

> The Master was once asked by his disciple, "What is the Buddha?"
>
> He replied, "The mind is the Buddha."
>
> Another day he was asked the same question. He replied, "No mind. No Buddha."
>
> The disciple protested, "But the other day you said, 'The mind is the Buddha.'"
>
> The Master said, "That was to stop the baby crying. When the baby stops crying, I say, 'No mind. No Buddha.'"[3]

The "baby is crying" in this man. His drive to control, to possess, to be the salvific center of his own self is so strong that all he can hear is what feeds into that compulsion. If Jesus slowly and gently spells out the commandments, the baby may stop crying long enough for the man to hear Jesus.

What Jesus wants him to hear is what Jesus has previously said but which he has not heard: "Why do you question me about what is good? There is One who is good." This is the second and deeper level of the recitation of the commandments. Jesus, the alert Master, always begins where the would-be disciple is in order to bring him to another place.

In the first exchange, Jesus took the question and with the man's own words changed the question. The man missed this change and asked for specific commandments. If he asks the teacher for specific commandments, specific commandments he will receive. But they will be given him in such a way that he may be led, if he follows the clues, to the realization that his question needs to be reformulated.

The key to Jesus' strategy is his choice of commandments. They all deal with the relationship to neighbor, ending with the very complex and limitless injunction to love your neighbor as yourself. What is missing are the commandments in relationship to God. Jesus has told this young man only the second of the two tablets of the law and only the second of the double commandment to love. This is strange, for in Jesus' way of life it is the loving relationship to God which provides the capacity to love the neighbor.

Our speculation is that he wanted the man to come to the realization that he had failed these commandments. If he came to this realization, he might have exclaimed, "Then who can be saved?" This is the correct question, the question that opens the human heart toward God. And it is the question which will eventually be asked, but not before the Master and the man have separated and Jesus has uttered his most consciousness-shattering proverb.

This is the question that would bring the man to the God of forgiving love and not the God of imposed demands. This would bring him into contact with the commandments glaringly missing from Jesus' recital, the first tablet of the law and the first and great commandment of love of God. He would then understand that whatever good he had accomplished was ultimately empowered by divine goodness, and he would enter everlasting life where human and divine energy interpenetrate one another. He would no longer pit himself against God's law for either honor or disgrace, for filled with life from the source of life, the boast of honor and the fear of disgrace disappear. If only, in honest scrutiny, he would cry out, "Then who can be saved?"

But that is not what he says. Instead he says, "I have kept all these. What do I need to do further?" We are now told, for the first time in Matthew's account, that this is a young man. He would have to be very young indeed to have kept all the commandments, for anyone with any length of days knows the truth of Eleanor's remark in *Lion in Winter:* "We broke all ten commandments on the spot." There is a brashness and bravado to his boast of obedience. It sounds too cavalier and self-justifying. It seems to have been said with the same speed and panic as "Which ones?" The ego is in the ascendancy, and the ego soars only on the wings of deceit.

After he has boldly stated that he is perfect (a self-judgment Jesus will ironically pick up on), he quickly returns to his basic posture of acquisitiveness. "What do I need to do further?" So far his entire system of reference is his own ego. Jesus' strategy of naming the commandments has neither calmed him nor brought him to the cry for mercy which is the common and truthful lot of humanity.

He has swallowed the Torah whole. This young man has a voracious heart, and the more he devours, the hungrier he is. In his present state of spirit, there is no chance he can "enter into" life. Quite simply, he is trying to take what can only be received. The overall portrait of this man is that he is sincere but self-preoccupied, energetic but spiritually obtuse.

This understanding of him contrasts with the standard appraisal that he is at an advanced stage of Hebrew spirituality. He has mastered the commandments, and Jesus is about to offer him the new and more perfect way of Christian discipleship. He is on a plateau looking for a peak. Our rendition sees this young man as impervious to the Master's art of apprenticeship. He is wrongheaded from his first question on, deaf to Jesus' attempts at correction, and rushing headlong down a path that does not lead to life. He is seriously deluded, and the Master must stop this "flow of delusion."

> Jesus told him, "If you seek perfection, go, sell your possessions, and give to the poor. You will then have treasure in heaven. Afterward, come back and follow me."
>
> Hearing these words, the young man went away sad, for his possessions were many.

Jesus plays upon his sincerity while trying to enlighten his obtuseness. "If you seek perfection" is a summary of this man's desire. To use a Shakespearean and perhaps too violent image, it is his own "petard that he will be hoisted on." "Go, sell your possessions, and give to the poor" is an exact reversal of this man's psychic energy. He has come to Jesus to increase his possessions. For him perfection is the acquiring of everlasting life. Jesus is telling him that perfection means relinquishing possessions and, more deeply, rooting out the whole spirit of seizure and holding.

It is helpful to note that Jesus has not suddenly introduced the question of possessions. This is what the conversation has been about from the beginning. This man's basic "take and hold" attitude extended even to God. He wanted to "possess everlasting life" and thereby, subtly but effectively, reverse the creator-creature relationship. He wishes to use his own goodness to make a legal claim on God's power. To Jesus, a Jew of the First Commandment, this is a life-destroying attitude which must be changed.

These words of Jesus to the young man and his response play upon the parables of the pearl and the treasure (Mt. 13:44–46). These parables, which are meant to suggest the advent of the Kingdom in people's lives, concern finding something of great value, going away and selling everything, and returning to buy the thing of great value (the pearl and the field in which the treasure is buried). In the parable of the treasure, we are given the interior state of the finder. He goes away and with joy sells all he has.

These two parables depict successful entries into the Kingdom. Similar dynamics—find, sell, buy—are present in Jesus' interaction with the young man. But there is a crucial change in the sequence. The young man is told to sell in order to find. If he sells his possessions, then he will have "treasure in heaven." This should not be seen as substituting the spiritual for the material, the things of heaven for the things of earth. If this were the case, there would be no change in the young man's basic spirit. In J. D. Salinger's novel *Franny and Zooey,* Zooey states that problem powerfully:

> . . . as a matter of simple logic, there's no difference at all, that I can see, between the man who's greedy for material treasure—or even intellectual treasure—and the man who's greedy for spiritual treasure. As you say, treasure's treasure, God damn it, and it seems to me that ninety percent of all the world-hating saints in history were just as acquisitive and unattractive, basically, as the rest of us are.[4]

Jesus is not recommending a different object of acquisition. He is stating that as long as the human spirit is acquisitive, it cannot enter everlasting life. If he disposes of his possessions, he will find the treasure of heaven. After this find, he is to return to Jesus and completely invest. "Afterward, come back and follow me." There is little doubt that the guide to the pearl of great price and treasure buried in the field is Jesus.

This change from "find, sell, buy" to "sell, find, buy" reflects the spiritual state of the young man. His problem is that his possessive spirit will not allow him to find what he is searching for. He must first divest himself in order to find the reality he wishes to invest himself in. He cannot find anything, for he is too busy seizing everything. His entry into life must begin with purgation. The hard saying is this: What you want you may not have because of the way you want it.

There is nothing wrong with seeking. It is seeking to possess that blocks the entry into life. The young man goes away sad, for he cannot go away glad. He has found nothing that might give him the impetus to sell everything. It is often stressed in the parable of the treasure that the selling of everything should not be seen as dour sacrifice. What was found is of such surpassing value that the selling is done joyfully. This is not a begrudging sale but a joyous dispersal. This is not the case with this young man. His spiritual state, his deeply entrenched perception of himself as laying claim to what he wants, demands a different strategy.

"On hearing this . . . " He hears these words of Jesus. He has not heard the previous words. His deafness to Jesus' earlier attempts to correct him has forced these confronting words. This time the Master has gotten through; the moment of decision is upon this young man. But his possessions were many and the possessive spirit that acquired them too powerful. He goes away sad, bound by the twisted knot of sin.

The possessive spirit that motivates the young man to seek everlasting life makes it impossible for him to find it. In Mark's rendition of this story, right before Jesus issues his command of sell, find, buy, he looks at the young man with love. We will never understand the harshness of Jesus until we understand it as a form of love, as the necessary expression of his ardent desire for our entry into life.

> Jesus said to his disciples: "I assure you, only with difficulty will a rich man enter into the kingdom of God. I repeat what I said: it is easier for a camel to pass through a needle's eye than for a rich man to enter the kingdom of God."
>
> When the disciples heard this they were completely overwhelmed, and exclaimed, "Then who can be saved?"

The episode takes a new turn. Jesus has failed with the rich young man. So he turns to his disciples to make sure they understand what has happened and to address the same attitude in them that he attempted to address in the young man. His words are the language of intensification. He begins with a solemn "I assure you" and continues with "I repeat what I said."

But what follows these introductions is not exactly the same. Jesus prosaically states that a rich man will enter the Kingdom "only with difficulty" and then imaginatively ups the ante by envisioning a camel standing helplessly before the eye of a needle. What started out as a difficulty ends up an impossibility. This powerful utterance is meant to confound the disciples and bring out in the open the spiritual dilemma which Jesus perceives.

It works. The disciples are completely thunderstruck. Why? It is often mentioned that in Israel wealth was a sign of divine favor and that here it is being proposed as an almost insurmountable obstacle to entering the Kingdom. This reversal is what astonished them.

But what is happening between Jesus and his disciples is deeper than that. Their response is "Then who can be saved?" and not "How will the rich be saved?" They hear in Jesus' words something universal and not a warning reserved only for the wealthy. More to the point, they hear in Jesus' words something that undercuts their own efforts at salvation. The words do not refer to the rich young man but to them. "Then who can be saved?" translates into "How can we be saved?" The disciples feel they are in jeopardy.

> Jesus looked at them and said, "For man it is impossible; but for God all things are possible."

When Jesus looked at them, he is readying them for the "thrust home."[5] This is the point of all that has gone before. If it is heard and received, it will result in a new consciousness and a view of human life from within the Kingdom of God. It has been foreshadowed from the very beginning. Jesus' first corrective response to the young man was that he had connected goodness with himself and not with God. Therefore, he was in a position of asserting his goodness in order to win life. But the Kingdom of God is not stormed by an aggressive ego but received like a child. One can seek, but one cannot seek to possess. One must seek openness in order to receive.

But our attachment to our own efforts as the way to salvation is deeply rooted. Only when we are brought to the point of impossibility are we open to a new possibility. The disciples exclaim, "Then who can be saved?" They do not speculate about it or calmly inquire about it. They are personally involved; their whole being is brought to the edge where human impossibility is evident and divine possibility is only dimly surmised. Then Jesus tries to push them over that edge into the long, slow, frightening fall into divine grace. In that fall, we know how ravens fly and lilies grow and how the smallest of seeds is indestructible.

But the enlightenment of any moment passes and we return to the questions and concerns of our previous mode of consciousness. What happened in the "thrust home" needs to be deepened and stabilized: it must be extended into action and outlook. All that it means is not yet evident to us. It is certainly not evident to Jesus's most beloved foil—Peter.

> Then it was Peter's turn to say to him: "Here we have put everything aside to follow you. What can we expect from it?"

With Peter's question the story moves in a different but complementary direction. That this whole section is a "training session" in discipleship is shown in Matthew's phrasing: "Then it was Peter's turn." Peter is talking for the group. What they have just experienced has raised another question. The disciples have been brought to "one place" in their relationship to God. Now with that new perception, they must be brought to another place in their relationship with their neighbor. Just as the question of the rich young man was the catalyst to expose and correct one fundamental attitude, the question of Peter will be the catalyst to expose and correct another attitude.

Peter's statement and question reveal what, in my small world, is called Chicago spirituality: "Where's mine?" or, in Chicago Latin, *"Ubi est mea?"* Peter is living in the world of comparison and reward. He is contrasting the disciples to the rich young man. They gave up everything, and he gave up nothing. But Peter's question reflects an attitude remarkably similar to the young man's. What are we going to get for what we have done? The drive for reward is built deep into the structures of human consciousness. Jesus responds to this drive effulgently:

> Jesus said to them: "I give you my solemn word, in the new age when the Son of Man takes his seat

> upon a throne be fitting his glory, you who have followed me shall likewise take your places on twelve thrones to judge the twelve tribes of Israel. Moreover, everyone who has given up home, brothers or sisters, father or mother, wife or children or property for my sake will receive many times as much and inherent everlasting life."

The answer to "What will we get?" appears to be "everything." Jesus is excessive in expressing what awaits them. It is reminiscent of the abundant blessings bestowed on Job at the end of his trials: "Thus the LORD blessed the latter days of Job more than his earlier ones" (Jb. 42:12). Jesus paints a picture of political and familial fullness. But he does not emphasize the connection between their present sacrifice and their future reward. It is a solemnly assured promise, but it is not necessarily the outcome of their effort. Sacrifice and reward go together, but their exact relationship is not clear. There is a short dialogue that is instructive:

> The saint has a complaint and places it squarely before God. "You bring out the worst in people. You promise them rewards for serving. Therefore, they do not do it freely but out of the desire for recompense."
>
> "Rewards," said God, "I promise no rewards. But often I get carried away."

Reward in Christian theology is a result of people dynamically relating to the source and destiny of life. Caught up in the reality of God, they are filled and transformed by divine love. Every image that seeks to communicate this fullness is inadequate to describe its actuality. But this "reward" is the inevitable overflow of a life-giving relationship. This is the source of Jesus' exuberant and wild images of promise.

What is promised is the fact of reward. What is dangerous is the attitude we may take toward reward. When reward is seen as winning prizes from a reluctant God, we are mired in an attitude that is not energized by the power of the Kingdom. There are many negative effects of this attitude. But Jesus focuses on the most paradoxical and self-defeating of these effects.

In the Kingdom of God when reward is causally linked to effort, reward becomes punishment. Jesus hears this distortion in Peter's question, and so the conversation is not yet over. The Master will attempt to transpose Peter and his disciples into a story world and then bring them back to the actual world of their concern. Perhaps this process will help them see the spiritual dilemma of their hearts.

> "Many who are first shall come last, and the last shall come first.
>
> "The reign of God is like the case of the owner of an estate who went out at dawn to hire workmen for his vineyard. After reaching an agreement with them for the usual daily wage, he sent them out to his vineyard. He came out about midmorning and saw other men standing around the marketplace without work, so he said to them, 'You too go along to my vineyard and I will pay you whatever is fair. ' At that they went away. He came out again around noon and midafternoon and did the same. Finally, going out in the late afternoon he found still others standing around.
>
> "To these he said, 'Why have you been standing here idle all day?' "'No one has hired us,' they told him.

> "He said, 'You go to the vineyard too.'
>
> "When evening came the owner of the vineyard said to his foreman, 'Call the workmen and give them their pay, but begin with the last group and end with the first.'
>
> "When those hired late in the afternoon came up they received a full day's pay, and when the first group appeared they supposed they would get more; yet they received the same daily wage.
>
> "Thereupon they complained to the owner, 'This last group did only an hour's work, but you have put them on the same basis as us who have worked a full day in the scorching heat.'
>
> "'My friend,' he said to one in reply, 'I do you no injustice. You agreed on the usual wage, did you not? Take your pay and go home. I intend to give this man who was hired last the same pay as you. I am free to do as I please with my money, am I not? Or are you envious because I am generous?'
>
> "Thus the last shall be first and the first shall be last."

This parable has been interpreted in many different ways in the course of Christian history. It has generated perspectives on salvation history, salvation and the life span of the individual, the priority of grace, the sovereignty of God, and the relationship between work done in this world and reward in the next.

But the context of our interpretation is Peter's unblushing combination of self-pity and self-interest—"Here we have put aside everything to follow you. What can we expect?"—and

Jesus' overwhelming "many times as much" assurance of fulfillment. The lack and emptiness which Peter feels is met by abundance. It is like a man with empty nets suddenly finding them filled with fish.

But no sooner has Jesus promised them the "everything and more" that they had put aside (and, of course, one wonders just how much they had to put aside in the first place), then he takes it all away again. He has just effectively told them that they will be first and then he forthrightly tells them that the first will be last and the last will be first. What exactly this strange combination of assurance and warning means is unfolded in the parable. The whole section will end by repeating the proverb: "Thus the last shall be first and the first last." But by that time, it will not be a statement of reversal but a statement of elimination. The whole question of first and last is inappropriate when dealing with a gracious and energetic employer whose major enemy seems to be idleness.

For our purposes, the story is about the relationship of the "heat-of-the-day" workers and the employer. The eleventh-hour people act as catalysts. The employer is freewheeling and self-determining yet, in the final confrontation scene, surprisingly gentle and reflective. He is probably the brother of a certain man who had two sons. Also, the story spends some time telling us about this man through his actions. What he does is just strange enough to prepare us for the greater strangeness to come.

He goes out at dawn to hire workers and makes an agreement with them. He also goes out at nine, noon, and three, and tells people to go to his vineyard. But he does not make an agreement with these workers; he says only that he will be just. Finally, he returns at five (the eleventh hour of a twelve-hour day); he asks people why they are idle and, upon hearing that no one has hired them, sends them also into his vineyard.

With these last people he neither makes an agreement nor says he will be just. Much of the motivation of this employer is left in the dark. Why did he keep going back to the marketplace? Did he need more workers than he hired the first time? The hint attached to the eleventh-hour workers is that he does not like to see people standing around doing nothing. This employer keeps coming back to where the people are. But he does not deal with them the same way. He does what he wants, but as we will see, this is not arbitrary. He does not do "what he damn well pleases."

The all-day people are best called the "heat-of-the-day" workers, for that is how they designate themselves. We are not told as much about them as about the employer, but we are told enough. First, they have made an agreement for a full-day's pay. Second, when they saw the eleventh-hour workers receiving a full-day's pay, they "supposed they would get more." This is the insight into how they see themselves. Third, when they receive what they had agreed upon, they grumble. Fourth, their complaint to the employer is not that they should get more money.

If anyone has lost out on this day's work, it is the employer. He is paying much more than he needs to pay. The pain of the heat-of-the-day workers is that the employer has made the last equal to themselves, who are the first. They know themselves only in comparison with others. Their identity is not formed in the originality of their own agreement with the employer but in envious competition with the other workers. This attitude is causing their grumbling and unhappiness.

The employer will point this out to them. He wants them to see it as he sees it, and so he employs a questioning approach with hopes to elicit their understanding and approval. "You agreed on the usual wage, did you not? I am free to do with my money as I please, am I not?" These are nondebatable questions. So what is the problem? The employer has a suggestion. It is put in the form of a question but it has all the revelatory power of a "thrust home." "Or are you envious because I am generous?"

This, of course, is precisely the problem, and the strange, unpredictable behavior of the employer has surfaced it. If we consider other possible responses to what happened, the pain of the heat-of-the-day workers is more clearly focused. They could have laughed and said, "God, that guy is screwy. He paid more than he had to. I wonder what he's up to?" Or they could have rejoiced at the good fortune of the eleventh-hour crowd and said, "What a lucky break! Let's head for the pub." Or they could have been clearheaded and said, "He's been fair with me. I've got no complaint." But they grumbled, for the envious condition of their heart selected from their experience those elements which would promote their unhappiness.

But we should not be too quick to let the employer off the hook. Throughout the story, he is portrayed as a transcendent figure whose actions emerge out of an interior freedom. He cheats no one, but neither does he explain why he treats some in this way and others in that way. All he explains about himself is that he is good and has a right to give what he has in ways that seem appropriate to him. This does not solve the problem of the envious heart, but it clearly states the conditions within which the envious heart must find healing. There will be no accommodation to their grumbling. The hard saying is that this is how God is—make of your life what you can.

There is an exchange in the resurrection narratives of John (Jn. 21:15–22) which makes a similar point but makes it a little more sharply. The risen Christ has confronted Peter ("Do you love me?"); commissioned Peter ("Feed my sheep"); predicted his future death; and ended with a simple "Follow me."

He has assured Peter, but Peter turns around and notices the disciple whom Jesus loved.

> Seeing him, Peter was prompted to ask Jesus, "But Lord, what about him?"
>
> "Suppose I want him to stay until I come," Jesus replied, "how does that concern you? Your business is to follow me."

We are stuck with our own uniqueness in relationship to the ultimate Mystery of life, and questions about why someone else appears to be treated better will be answered with "How does that concern you? Your business is to follow me." This is a terribly unsatisfying limit, and so we create theology.

But what has this parable done for Peter and the disciples? They have been transposed into its world, and now they must return to their own. Jesus heard in their statement and question ("Here we have put everything aside to follow you. What can we expect from it?") the same attitude that made the heat-of-the-day workers grumble and complain. The point to the disciples is that they will get everything and enjoy nothing. All they ever wanted will be theirs: they will inherit the Kingdom.

But because other people who have not sacrificed as much as they have will also inherit the Kingdom, they will not be able to be happy. They are gauging themselves in relationship to the rich young man who went away. They understand their entering into life only in relationship to his walking away from it. Their worth is dependent on his lack of it and not on their originality in relationship to God's plan. This places them in a position that is not completely without irony. They will receive everything and enjoy nothing.

This whole "training session" in Matthew has been about how the disciples must respond to the goodness of God. It begins with Jesus stating firmly that God alone is good, a conviction that causes difficulties for both the rich young man and the disciples. The section ends with the employer stating that his goodness has caused the heat-of-the-day workers to be envious, literally to have an "evil eye." This is something we do not often ponder. We applaud the goodness of God because it is the foundation of our salvation. But we do not often consider it as the source of our consternation.

The convictions of Christian faith demand that the disciples readjust their attitudes, and some of these attitudes are deeply rooted in personal and cultural assumptions. If they are readjusted, a new future becomes possible, but it is a future that combines equal measures of terror and promise. It is an "old saw" but true nonetheless: faith causes as many problems as it solves. Or more creatively put, it orients the person so radically that it changes the tasks and struggles of life.

We have watched the Master at work. Perhaps as he has been questioning, affirming, confronting, and transposing his scriptural disciples, he has also been guiding his contemporary followers into the perspectives and attitudes of life in the Kingdom. We could sum up the wisdom about success, joy, and divine handwriting; about leaving fear to the hair-counting God; about the staunch goodness of God which refuses the territorial claim of humans and which will not become part of the futile game of worth by comparison.

We could also continue with other gospel stories. We could catch Jesus angry and ironical as he eats with the Pharisees and tells them about another banquet which they most desperately want to go to but which they perversely will not be able to attend (Lk. 14:1–24). Or we could see the patient-pushing-passionate Master teach his disciples not to dismiss hunger down the road but to sit it on green grass

(Mk. 6:34–44; 8:1–9). The Gospels are a source book about how to live and die according to the way of Jesus.

But when the wisdom of the way of Jesus is abstracted from the concrete interaction between himself and people, it becomes platitude. Platitude is not so much a banal truth as any truth divorced from the dynamics of life which gave it birth. Wisdom will always emerge from an encounter with Jesus, but this wisdom will never substitute for the actual encounter. It is not the wisdom itself that is important, but the wisdom as it shapes the raw material of a person's life. As long as Jesus is always considered from this essential interpersonal perspective, he remains the Master. When he is reduced to a message which can be passed out on the corner, the teacher hides and the tongue that can rouse the weary is silenced.

Part Three

Friendship

CHAPTER SEVEN

Friendship with the Master

When we find something out, we want to tell somebody. There is nothing worse than to be bursting with news and not be able to find an ear to spill it in. After the old Anna saw the child Jesus, she "talked about the child to all who looked forward to the deliverance of Jerusalem" (Lk. 2:38). And of course, if it is a secret, there is even more delight in publishing it. Jesus once told his disciples that he was fulfilling a prophesy which foretold "I will open my mouth in parables, I will announce what has lain hidden since the creation of the world" (Mt. 13:35).

There is more than a little irony in this remark. Parables may be revelatory, but they are seldom clear. What has been hidden since the creation of the world often remains hidden after the parable has been spoken. But there is still the need to say what you have discovered. So another story is told.

When we enter into a gospel episode or saying and the Master teaches us, we need to respond. As we mentioned, the fullest response is action. But we can also ponder and talk reflectively about what happened. A third option is that we can imaginatively respond. Some people compose music, others paint, still others, I'm told, dance. I am addicted to poetry and stories. It is one of the ways I respond to the "training sessions" of the Master. From an objective standpoint, the stories may be good or bad, have some literary quality or be innocent of all art. But from my point of view, I feel I do not understand the way of Jesus until I am able to tell a story which embodies the twists and turns of life that he has taught me.

This section is called "friendship" for a friend knows something of what the Master knows. The Master, of course, remains the Master. "Only one is your teacher" (Mt. 23:10). But we all get insights, now and then, into the way of Jesus. A Jesus story or saying leaps out at us and tells us something that brings life. This is the work of the *inspired imagination* of sacred Scripture. When our eyes are opened and our ears unstopped, our mouth is also loosed. We speak back to what first spoke to us. This is the *answering imagination.* We should not be surprised at all to see that friendship flourishes in conversation.

The Father of Ice Cream

The Inspired Imagination

> Jesus said, "What father among you will give his son a snake if he asks for a fish, or hand him a scorpion if he asks for an egg?"
>
> Luke 11:11–12

The Answering Imagination

> Tom, eleven, was the first in the door at 31 Flavors. He announced to everyone in the store, "I get the window on way back."
>
> Alice, the oldest at thirteen, followed. She was somewhere between dolls and nylons and she looked like she would rather be anywhere but where she was. Next Janet, who was nine, was shoved through the door by Jeff, who was aggressively eight. Next came the biggest of the group, a man by the name of Daddy, who was holding the hand of the smallest of the group, a boy by the name of Paul.

They all lined up in front of the plateglass wonderland. "Whatever you want," said the father. His arms spread out, indicating all 31 flavors.

"I want a scoop of rocky road and licorice in a cup," grinned Jeff, the eight-year-old.

"Daddy, Daddy, Daddy!" Janet, the nine-year-old, was sputtering. "That's what I was going to get. I told Jeff in the car that I was going to get that. That's why he got it."

"Janet, I'm sure they have enough rocky road and licorice for two," the great mediator assured her. She glared at her father.

Meanwhile, Tom had conned the teenage girl behind the counter into giving him a taste of pralines 'n' cream and double chocolate. He was now pushing along into banana fudge and pineapple swirl.

"Tom!" shouted his father. Tom backed off and returned the little pink tasting spoon to the girl. His father said only one word, but the communication was unmistakable. They had had the conversation before.

"Daddy," said Alice in a refined voice, "I'll have two scoops of lime sherbet in a cup." She got her ice cream and drifted away from her embarrassing family toward a group of teenagers in the corner.

Paul, the five-year-old, had said, "Daddy," three times and tugged vigorously on his father's pants before he looked down. "I want bubblegum peppermint."

"Don't get the bubblegum peppermint," coaxed his father. "You like chocolate chip."

"I want peppermint bubblegum." Paul's voice moved toward tears.

"OK. But you're going to finish it," said the father, doing his imitation of a stern parent.

The father turned back to Janet, who was pouting in the corner. "What'll you have, honey?"

"Vanilla." Her voice was as cold as the ice cream.

Jeff said, "Boy, this rocky road and licorice is good."

"Jeff!" said the father. It was the same one-word conversation he had had with Tom. Jeff walked away.

The father bent down for a private conversation with Janet. "Janet, honey, don't cut off your nose to spite your face. Get the rocky road and licorice."

She looked at her father as if he were the dumbest man on the face of the earth. He knew nothing about life. "Vanilla in a plain cone," she said adamantly. She would not be denied the wrong done to her.

Tom was pacing up and down in front of the glassed-in choices.

"You'll have to make up your mind," said his father.

"OK. I'll have a hot fudge banana split with four scoops of ice cream—chocolate, double chocolate, chocolate chip, and chocolate ripple."

"No extra nuts?" suggested the father.

"Extra nuts!" said Tom excitedly.

"And two maraschino cherries for my son," added the father.

"I don't like this bubblegum peppermint," came a voice from the floor.

"Give it to me, Paul," said the father. "And give him a scoop of chocolate chip in a plain cone." The teenage girl behind the counter hurried it up.

The father licked the bubblegum peppermint. He didn't like it either.

Then out of the wealth of his pockets, Daddy paid for it.

The father was herding his children out the door when Alice, his oldest, said, "Daddy, I'm going to stay with these kids I met."

He looked over at the teenagers in the corner with that steely parental appraisal that withers all wrongdoing.

"Be home by five." He was startled by the tenderness in his voice.

From outside came Tom's voice. "I said I have the window on the way home."

The father turned immediately and pushed out the door, for his children needed him.

The Mother of Soda Bread

The Inspired Imagination

> Jesus went on: "To what shall I compare the reign of God? It is like yeast which a woman took to knead into three measures of flour until the whole mass of dough began to rise."
>
> Luke 13:20–21

The Answering Imagination

Sarah had to have it. Not just for herself. Her children, neighbors, and friends "oohed and aahed" over it, and everyone urged her to find out how to make it before it was too late. Her mother was getting up in years and it would be a shame if it went with her. So she waited for the right moment and spoke with studied casualness.

"Ma, mind if I watch you make the soda bread and take a few notes?"

"Why should I?" said her mother and slurped her tea loudly.

I'll never break her of that habit, thought Sarah.

The next afternoon Ma gathered on the countertop all the ingredients necessary for her family-and-neighborhood famous soda bread—flour, sugar, raisins, butter, and a host of ancient spice bottles that were hidden in the back of the cabinet. Then with a deep intake of breath like a conductor the second before a symphony, she began.

Sarah took copious notes. Each pinch and dab and sprinkle were scribbled on her yellow pad. Later on, looking over her jottings, she was puzzled by the entry "HDE." Then she remembered. That was shorthand for "hit dough with elbow." For the truth was that abbreviations were needed. When Sarah's mother began to make the bread, she seemed to go into a trance. She moved gracefully around the kitchen and her hands were as swift and precise as a concert pianist's. Sarah had all she could do to keep up.

The next day, Sarah taped her notes to the cabinet door and began meticulously to follow the instructions. When she came to the part about elbowing the dough, she looked around to make sure she was alone. She felt a little silly, but then delivered the dough a mighty blow. No pro basketball player ever threw a better elbow.

That night at dinner she presented the bread with all the anxiety of a bride's first meal. Her family praised the soda bread extravagantly but unanimously agreed that it was not as good as Grandma's.

That made Sarah more determined than ever, and sent her back for a second note-taking session.

The next afternoon, her mother began her ritual of baking. Everything was as Sarah had marked it down. She could not see where she had gone wrong.

"Ma, I did everything just as you did, but it didn't turn out the same."

"You forgot the yeast," her mother said.

"You don't use yeast in soda bread," said Sarah.

"You use yeast in everything," instructed her mother.

"I didn't see you use it."

"When I was kneading the dough, I saw all the faces of all

the people who would eat it. That yeast entered the dough and made it bread."

"What are you?" said Sarah, laughing. "Some kind of bread mystic?"

Her mother smiled. But she did not deny it.

The Daughter of Christmas

The Inspired Imagination

> "Let this be a sign to you: in a manger you will find an infant wrapped in swaddling clothes."
>
> Luke 2:12

The Answering Imagination

The Christmas tree is a towering beauty. It drips with tinsel, bursts with ornaments, and is strung with technicolor lights. Under the tree is a large crib set. Joseph and Mary, Wise Men and shepherds, sheep and camels—all have their eyes on the baby Jesus. The eyes of baby Jesus, however, are looking up and out into the living room, where the entire family has gathered to exchange gifts.

A present is passed to the uncle first. Over the years the family has learned that Christmas is more pleasant if he is first to open a gift.

"Mine?" he grins and attacks the box. He wrestles the brightly colored wrappings free, muscling them into a sphere which he basketballs toward the trash bag. Then he forces the box open and sizes up the white shirt and red tie.

"Needed" is his one-word appraisal. "Who do I have to thank for this?" The card was lost in the carnage.

Next a gift arrives at the lap of his niece who is twelve. She opens the card and reads each line carefully, as painstakingly as a biblical scholar.

"Oh, thank you!" she exclaims. It is from her grandmother.

In one bound she is across the room with a flurry of kisses and a hug.

"You better check it out first," her uncle suggests. "You never know. It could be socks."

She does not hear him. She is back at the box. As carefully as a mother unwraps the blanket in which a baby is cradled, she unfastens and folds the green paper.

"Going to save it?" her uncle chides. This ceremony is tedious to him. His eye drifts to a big box near the door.

"Green is one of my favorite colors and Grandma knew that when she picked it out. Besides, you can always use pretty paper."

The box reveals a green sweater with a sky of white stars in the upper half from shoulder to shoulder.

The uncle watches his niece shriek with delight, cover her grandmother with a second round of kisses, and disappear into her room.

"Could we continue opening the presents while she's trying on the sweater?" the uncle said and gave an exasperated and adult shrug of his shoulders like a man who has been burdened with too much common sense.

But before anyone could answer his plea for speed, his niece returned wearing her new sweater and spun around for all to see.

"O thank you," she said. It sounded like a song.

No one noticed the Christmas tree.

Twenty Into Fifty Goes a Hundredfold

The Inspired Imagination

> People were bringing their little children to him to have him touch them, but the disciples were scolding them for this. Jesus became indignant when he

> noticed it and said to them: "Let the children come to me and do not hinder them."
>
> Mark 10:13–14

The Answering Imagination

Big Jerry groaned when his wife told him he had to go to the store. It was the Wednesday before Thanksgiving and the grocery store would be Grand Central Station. But when he heard that one of the missing ingredients was cranberry sauce, he nodded reluctantly.

"How could you forget cranberry sauce?" he muttered.

But when his wife yelled from the upstairs bedroom, "Take Little Jerry with you," Big Jerry knew how she could forget cranberry sauce. This was all part of a bigger plot.

Lately, Big Jerry's wife had been on his case. He wasn't spending enough time with his son. "He needs you, Gerard." Always "Gerard" when there was a lesson to be given. "Just because he's gotten older, that doesn't mean you two have to be so far apart. He's only eleven, you know." Always "you know" when she thought he didn't know. Big Jerry did not like these chiding lectures. It made him feel that he was a bit of a fool, and anyone who had done as well as he had in business was no fool.

Big Jerry stuck his head into the den.

"Want to go to the store?"

Little Jerry buttoned the television dead and was at his father's heels.

Big Jerry knew that sometime tomorrow Little Jerry's mother would probe, "What did you and Jerry talk about when you went to the store?" She was hoping for something significant, like the facts of life or the value of a buck.

So Big Jerry tried to get a conversation going.

"How's school?"

"OK."

"How's your basketball team doing?"

"Lousy."

"What were you watching on TV?"

"A movie."

Big Jerry put his foot on the gas. This is normal, he thought to himself; this is normal.

At the store the cranberry sauce, five cans, was scooped up. Big Jerry had feared they might be out of it. They also found the lettuce, nuts, diet Coke, pie-crust mix, rolls, orange juice, and something called nutmeg.

When they turned out of the last aisle, they saw the people. The line at the "Under Ten" checkout counter was over ten people long.

"Grand Central Station," muttered Big Jerry.

"What?" asked Little Jerry.

"Lot of people."

"Yeah."

The checker was a teenage boy, and he was carrying on a conversation with the neighboring checker, a teenage girl. It was about a party both had been to and both had hated. To Big Jerry's ears every other word was "boring" and "really."

More work and less talk, thought Big Jerry. He noticed the other people in line were giving each other exasperated looks. Big Jerry began to mumble under his breath. He noticed the checker had a bad case of acne.

By the time they got to the front, Big Jerry was steaming. But he said nothing. He just put a fifty-dollar bill on the counter.

The checker, happily gabbing away, rang up a $19.35 charge. When Big Jerry saw how much it was, he picked up his fifty and put down a twenty.

The checker did not notice the switch, and gave him $30.65 in change. Big Jerry hesitated. This kid deserves to be taken, he thought. Little Jerry was at his side.

"I gave you a twenty," Big Jerry said.

"No you didn't. You gave me a fifty."

"I gave you a twenty."

"I saw the fifty," the checker insisted.

"Look in the drawer!" Big Jerry's words came out as a growl between clenched teeth.

The checker checked. "Oh yeah." He took all but the sixty-five cents back.

In the parking lot a man came up behind Big Jerry and his son. "You should have taken that jerk for the thirty."

In the car, Little Jerry said to his father, "That was neat, Dad." And he began to talk—about school, about basketball, about the movie he was watching on TV.

Big Jerry tried to listen, but he didn't hear much for three insights, in rapid succession, raked his mind.

If Little Jerry hadn't been there, he would have grabbed the thirty and walked.

His wife was wrong. Little Jerry didn't need him; he needed Little Jerry.

And he was glad tomorrow was Thanksgiving.

Shenanigans At Cana

The Inspired Imagination

> At a certain point the wine ran out, and Jesus' mother told him, "They have no more wine."
>
> Jesus replied, "Woman, how does this concern of yours involve me? My hour has not yet come."
>
> His mother instructed those waiting on table, "Do whatever he tells you."
>
> John 2:3–5

John Shea

The Answering Imagination

"Come now, my Son,
do you tease these gray hairs?
Late and laughing you arrive and find me finding you.
An entreaty is my greeting.
'They have no more wine.'
But you sweep me up
in mock debate,
a young man's arms
around my seriousness,
wresting from me a conspiratorial smile.
'What has that to do with me?'
you say,
winking words which invite the memory of our meals.
And I tell you quick,
in hushes,
how
I lit the fire in your eyes
and held your head of dreams
and poured water in your hands
when you came burning
from the desert sands.
Beyond that,
I say,
you and I
are strangers,
I say.
But games aside,
I say,
Jesus,
I say,
These empty glasses mock your father's feast.

'My hour is not yet come,'
you say,
making me say it all
right here
in the midst of sober guests.
You hold me now
in roles reversed,
a son giving birth
a mother young again.
Steward,
I say,
this man who kisses my eyes,
this Son of my love
has need of a canyon
to hold the grapes
that his fast feet
will crush to marriage wine.
Now,
the teeth of our laughter
blinds the steward
who does not know
what we do,
my secret friend.
Your hour is the minute
the wine fails.

The Penny Planter

The Inspired Imagination

Jesus said, "Listen carefully to this. A farmer went out sowing. Some of what he sowed landed on the footpath, where the birds came along and ate it. Some of the seed landed on rocky ground where it had little soil; it sprouted immediately because the

> soil had no depth. Then, when the sun rose and scorched it, it began to wither for lack of roots. Again, some landed among thorns, which grew up and choked it off, and there was no yield of grain. Some seed, finally, landed on good soil and yielded grain that sprang up to produce at a rate of thirty- and sixty—and a hundredfold."
>
> Mark 4:3–8

The Answering Imagination

Patricia plants pennies.

She lives on Farmer Avenue. It is called Farmer Avenue because years ago it was the road the farmers took into town to sell their produce. It used to be a popular road. The adults would pull their wagons over to the side and talk, catching up on the news, hugging friends not seen for some time, and making dates and deals. The children would run and play in the fields and sneak up behind the wagons and snitch apples and pears, carrots and tomatoes. Going to town was an excuse for a picnic.

Time and the new highway changed all that. Now Farmer Avenue is a quiet, tree-lined, residential section. Its only traffic is a morning and evening rush hour flow of men and women trying to catch or trying to escape from the buses which stop at the corner. These hassled, unsuspecting people are the special subjects of Patricia's ministrations.

Patricia is ten, and the initial burst of summer excitement at being out of school has faded. Although she fills her days with baseball and swimming, her nights with rock tapes, and as much time as she can with Tim Freemont, who was a grade ahead of her in school, she is bored—like totally. But her mother has put a lid on it. "Young lady, I don't want to hear you say one more time that you're bored." So Patricia locks the bathroom door and drones into the sympathetically listening mirror, "Boring! Boring!"

It was in this sorry state of soul that she began drawing arrows on the sidewalk. She started one house down from her own. With a large yellow chalk she scratched out an arrow and attached the message "TREASURE AHEAD." Then, three sidewalk squares later, a second arrow with the same message. Then, directly in front of her house, the arrow pointed sideways and the message changed to "TREASURE NEAR." Any eyes interested enough to follow the chalk arrow would see a large, very old oak tree that grew in the middle of Patricia's front yard. The trunk of the tree had split for the first time only four feet from the ground. In the flat space of this split, shinny as a newborn baby, lay a penny.

From the window of her room on the second floor Patricia could see it all.

No two people reacted the exact same way. Some people just stomped on by, like they never even noticed the signs they were stepping on.

Others briefly glanced down but were in too much of a hurry to follow the leads.

Some hesitated; their eyes followed the arrow to the tree; then their no-nonsense feet took them to the bus.

Some stood on the sidewalk for a while, then tiptoed across the grass toward the tree. When they found the penny in the nook, they flipped it in the air with a laugh and pocketed it.

One man picked it up, examined it like a rare coin collector, and put it back.

Each morning and evening Patricia would watch them and pray that the hurriers would stop, and the stoppers would seek, and the seekers would find, and the finders would rejoice, and she would get to sneak out of her house and plant another penny in the tree. The sheer stealth of it all delighted her so much that she completely abandoned her mirror conversations.

Patricia's favorite was a thin young man. He wore a three-piece suit and carried a brown attaché case, but that did not fool her. She knew that as soon as he reached home, he put on cutoffs and a T-shirt and shot baskets before dinner. The first day he strolled on by, not to be bothered. The second day he read the signs on the sidewalk. The third day he glanced at the tree. The fourth day he walked very slowly, genuflected to tie his shoelace, looked around to see who was watching, and then kept on going. The fifth day he ran by.

He needs help, thought Patricia.

And so she put her not inconsiderable mind to it. In fact it was what she was pondering right before bed when she looked out her window and saw a figure on the sidewalk. The blend of the streetlight and the leafy branches of the tree covered the figure in shadows. But she could see it was a thin young man in cutoffs and a T-shirt. She threw open her window and thundered, "Go for it!"

The young man stiffened as if he had been suddenly drenched by a storm he did not see coming. He turned and bolted down the sidewalk.

"I'll have to try something else," said Patricia out loud to whoever might be listening. "But make no mistake. I'm going to get him."

Star-Gazer

The Inspired Imagination

> Once, on being asked by the Pharisees when the reign of God would come, he replied: "You cannot tell by careful watching when the reign of God will come. Neither is it a matter of reporting that it is

> 'here' or 'there.' The reign of God is already in your midst."
>
> Luke 17:20–21

The Answering Imagination

Since his daughter was only three and too young to buy him a Father's Day gift, he purchased one for himself.

The telescope was magnificent. It was a "Discover Deluxe." It had three lenses building up to two hundred and twenty-seven magnification. It had a counterbalanced equatorial mounting and included a diagonal prism, sun projector screen, and an SLR reflex finder scope. The salesman threw in an accessory tray. Mounted on its tripod next to the window it was aimed like a rifle at the stars.

Every night after dinner the owner pasted his eye to the viewfinder and scanned the heavens for movement, excited over the patterns of light a million miles over his head.

At his feet his daughter played.

The Phone Call

The Inspired Imagination

> Jesus said, "If you bring your gift to the altar and there recall that your brother [or sister] has anything against you, leave your gift at the altar, go first and to be reconciled with your brother [or sister], and then come and offer your gift."
>
> Matthew 5:23–24

The Answering Imagination

"Ma, come to the table," Ellen said in a voice that betrayed nothing.

It was Christmas afternoon. The five Dolans—Tom and Ellen, their children Marge, Patrick, and Catlin—and Ellen's mother Marie McKenzie, had gone to church, opened presents, and lingered forever over a Christmas drink. Dinner was now on the table.

Marie said she was not hungry. She rocked back and forth in her favorite chair. On the table next to her was the phone.

"Ma, if she's going to call, she will call. Come to the table."

Marie just rocked.

Ellen gestured her husband Tom into the kitchen. "I spend all day on this meal, and she is letting it get cold. This is the thanks I get. All year I take care of her. Take her to bingo, the hairdresser's, church. And every holiday she sulks there waiting for that daughter of hers to call."

Tom had heard all this before. "I don't think she's sulking," said Tom. "I'll take care of it."

Tom went back into the living room, right past Marie at her telephone post, and up the stairs to their bedroom. Marie pretended she didn't see him.

Tom took their phone listings out of the dresser drawer and dialed the California number.

"Yeah!" said a groggy man's voice.

Oh no, thought Tom, not another one. "Is Ann there?"

"Minute."

"Hello."

"Ann, this is Tom. Merry Christmas. Call your mother."

"Tom, for Christ's sake, it's only noon out here. I'll call her later."

"Now, Ann. We can't get her to come to the table and eat. Ellen is doing a slow burn."

"So what's new?" She waited, but Tom said nothing. "OK. I'll call."

Tom was halfway down the stairs when the phone rang. Marie answered it on the second ring.

"Hi ya, Mom. Ellen feeding you enough?"

"Oh Annie, it's so good to hear your voice."

"Good to hear yours too, Mom. I went to midnight mass and was sleeping late." She reached under the covers and gave Hank a squeeze. He didn't move. He had fallen back to sleep.

"By the way, Mom, I got your check. Thanks. I needed it."

"You're welcome. When will you be in Chicago?"

"Spring sometime. I'll let you know."

"I miss you."

"You've got Ellen right there, Mom." Her voice got louder as if her mother were hard of hearing.

"Would you like to talk to her?"

There was a moment of silence. "Why not?"

"Here she is."

Ellen had been listening to each word from the kitchen doorway. She walked toward her mother wiping her hands on her apron. Marie held out the phone. The cord was stretched to the full.

Ellen took the phone. "Merry Christmas."

"Merry Christmas," returned Ann.

Ellen gave the phone back to her mother.

"There," Marie said to anyone who was listening. Her voice had a sense of accomplishment as if she had just carried a great weight up a forbidding hill and set it down right where it should be. "Merry Christmas," she said out loud to herself.

Then Marie puckered a kiss into the phone's receiver and said, "Bye, Annie, don't let the bedbugs bite."

"Oh, Mom," Ann managed before her mother hung up. Marie came immediately to the table. The children were stifling laughs; Tom was smiling; Ellen was staring at the plate.

They recited grace together. The food was passed and piled high on each plate.

Marie poured the tea into her cup, poured the tea from the cup onto her saucer, then blew on it to cool it off. A forkful of dressing went into her mouth.

"Delicious," she said with her mouth full.

"Oh, Mom," sighed Ellen.

Cro-Magnon Popcorn

The Inspired Imagination

> "Good measure pressed down, shaken together, running over, will they pour into the fold of your garment."
>
> Luke 6:38

The Answering Imagination

With the possible exception of Leonardo da Vinci airport in Rome during a ground crew strike, the popcorn counter at the Varsity five minutes before the beginning of *The Return of the Jedi* is the most hassled place on earth.

Behind the twenty-foot plateglass counter scurries a teenage girl. She is alone, struggling to respond to fifty pressing patrons. She is racing up and down the counter—diving for Raisinettes, dipping to fill a popcorn box, jamming a cup under the Coke dispenser. Her long blond hair is tied in a pony tail, and when she turns suddenly to fill an order, it lifts off her back like a kite.

Waiting in line is Robert, known affectionately to the other members of the football team as Cro-Magnon Man. When he finally reaches the front line of customers, he speaks two words. Thcy sound as if they were shouted into a canyon. "Large popcorn."

The frazzled girl scoops up the popcorn into the tub box, slams it on the counter, and moves on. But with the hard contact on the counter the popcorn, which appeared to fill the box, caves in. There had been a false bottom of air. Only three-quarters of a box of popcorn stares up at Cro-Magnon Man.

A sound emits from Robert, a primitive, guttural cry of pain as if the tusk of a wild boar had torn into his leg.

The patrons turn in terror, sure the end is upon them. The counter girl stops in her tracks, looks back, and immediately sizes up the situation. She grabs the popcorn scoop, loads it with popcorn, and upturns it over Robert's box. The popcorn fills the box, brims over, and spills onto the countertop.

"Here, monster!" says the girl, laughing.

Robert utters a second sound, a low purr of pleasure as if someone infinitely larger than he was had reached down and petted him.

Martha The Good

The Inspired Imagination

> On their journey Jesus entered a village where a woman named Martha welcomed him to her home. She had a sister named Mary, who seated herself at the Lord's feet and listened to his words. Martha, who was busy with all the details of hospitality, came to him and said, "Lord, are you not concerned that my sister has left me to do the household tasks all alone? Tell her to help me."
>
> The Lord in reply said to her: "Martha, Martha, you are anxious and upset about many things; one thing only is required."
>
> Luke 10:38–41

The Answering Imagination

Martha is as good as a butter cookie. The Good Samaritan could take lessons from her. If someone is sick, she is first down the block with a meal and chatter. "If you need anything just let me know." She means it.

But her mothering is never neglected. After dinner with the dishes cleared, she sits with her two daughters at the kitchen table and helps them with their homework. She guides Janet, who is fourteen, through the maze of algebra. Next she listens to Alice, her fifth grader, spell the ever-elusive "b-o-u-q-u-e-t."

When the girls are finished and off in their own room, she joins her husband before the television set. "They're doing well," she says with a nod.

"They have a good helper," Tom says.

Martha's husband, Tom, is proud of her. He basks in her goodness. She likes it when she can feel him feeling good about her. It gives her the support she needs to go on.

Martha is also socially concerned. She deplores media hype, government lies, big-business ploys. She cannot understand the cruelty and apathy everyone seems to take for granted. At the center of it all, she tells whoever will listen, is rampant self-interest.

"No one cares for anyone but themselves," she says, mounting her soapbox.

"Martha to the rescue," chides Tom.

"Well, they don't," she insists, calming down a bit. She is determined she will not be that way.

Her parish staffs a soup kitchen in the downtown district. The name of the kitchen is Nazareth. One night a week Martha and her oldest daughter go down there and prepare sandwiches and soup for whoever comes in off the street. While the street people are eating, Martha and Janet clean the kitchen. When the street people are done and gone, mother and daughter straighten up and head for home. On their "social action" night, Tom cooks and has dinner waiting for them. The conversation usually goes the same way.

"How many tonight?" Tom asks.

"About ten," Martha answers.

"It's a good work."

"It's little enough."

"It's a lot."

"I feel sorry for them."

"You should."

"I guess so."

One Tuesday night at 11:30 the doorbell rang. "Who could that be at this hour?" Tom said as he got out of bed to answer it.

"Oh my God!" Martha heard Tom say. She put on her robe and went to the door.

It was Tom's father. The last time they had seen him was at the wedding seventeen years ago. He was drunk then too.

"Martha, honey," he smiled, and gave her a hug. Liquor had wasted him. When he grinned, all the bones of his face showed.

The first night he slept on the couch. But by the end of the week the den had been turned into a temporary bedroom. He would sleep away the days and prowl at night. Whatever liquor was in the house always disappeared.

It was Alice, the youngest, who said it: "Gee, Mom. We have our own personal street person."

Martha was not amused. "Tom, how long is he going to stay?" Her voice had an edge to it.

"He's my father. I can't just throw him out," Tom snapped. Then he playfully grabbed and rubbed the back Martha's neck. "Give me time," he pleaded.

A month passed and Tom had not found the time.

One night at supper, after the girls had left the table, the family street person slurred, "That Janet of yours is really growing into a ripe young woman."

That night in bed Martha said, "He has to go."

"As soon as I can." Tom turned toward the wall.

Two days later they found him on the floor of the den. The ambulance got him to the hospital in time. The heart attack was not fatal.

He had no insurance. Tom and Martha dug into their savings for a two-week hospital stay. When he was released, they rented a hospital bed. The den was rearranged to a permanent sickroom. And Martha the good became full-time nurse to a cranky, unappreciative, foul-mouthed old man.

One afternoon he yelled from his bed, "Goddamnit, Martha, bring me a beer."

In the kitchen Martha stood perfectly still. Her voice was a whispered monotone, but her ears heard what her mouth said: "God, I hope the son of a bitch dies." Her whole heart was in every word.

And it was as if she had caught God in a rare moment when he had nothing to do but listen. And as a reward for her years of goodness, he tickled her father-in-law's heart into thrombosis and left her staring into the coffin with her answered prayer, wondering how she would ever get back to the garden now that she lived so far east of Eden.

The day of the funeral was also Martha's "social action" night.

"Stay home, tonight," Tom said.

"I'm going," Martha said. Her teeth were clenched.

She and Janet opened Nazareth and prepared the soup and sandwiches. But she did not clean the kitchen while the street people ate. For some reason she still does not understand, she sat at the table with a bowl of soup.

Tears came with the first taste and did not stop. But she finished the soup like a medicine she had long avoided.

On the way home in the car her daughter asked, "You OK, Mom?"

The words came out slowly, with audible sighs between them, the result of some interior, labored birth.

"Next week we'll bring flowers for the tables. Maybe your father and sister will come with us. We'll all eat at Nazareth."

The Cigar Smoker

The Inspired Imagination

> Then Jesus took a little child, stood him in their midst, and putting his arms around him, said to them, "Whoever welcomes a child such as this for my sake welcomes me. And whoever welcomes me welcomes, not me, but him who sent me."
>
> Mark 9:36–37

The Answering Imagination

The Kingdom of God is like a cigar smoker without his cigar.

The cigar smoker was giving a workshop in Los Angeles. It began in glory and ended in humiliation. At the close, people were grumbling, and his departure was more in the nature of an escape. But as the cab dragged through traffic to the airport, he thought to himself, "If only I can get to the airport, get on the plane, nurse a double martini, eat whatever lousy food the airline is serving, and smoke my cigar, everything will be all right." For this was many years ago when cigar smoking on airplanes was allowed.

For the first time in three days there were no hitches. He got to the airport, got on the plane, and plunked himself down in an aisle seat in the smoking section.

Next to him in the middle seat was a little girl, around four years old. She had with her everything little girls carry on airplanes—a half-eaten bag of Fritos; a coloring book with a box of broken crayons; and a doll, mussed from too much hugging and squeezing. In the window seat sat the little girl's mother.

Los Angeles, as usual, was socked in, a thick mixture of fog and smog. As the plane left the ground, it entered the thick, gray clouds. The cabin darkened. But as the plane climbed, the cabin grew progressively lighter until the dazing moment when the plane broke out of the clouds into the sun.

The captain turned off the no-smoking sign. The woman in the window seat lit up a cigarette. When the cigar smoker looked over and saw her, his heart sank. As she inhaled the smoke, she waved her hand back and forth in front of her mouth. The smoke wafted upward and drifted toward the front of the cabin.

The cigar smoker instantly knew what this meant. This woman was going to smoke her cigarette, but there was going to be no smoke in the little girl's eyes. But the cigar smoker also knew that when he lit up his cigar, smoke would swirl through the cabin, infiltrate the cockpit, and seep out into the universe. And if he lit up his cigar, this little girl would be engulfed in smoke. She would be coughing her pathetic little-girl cough. People would be staring angrily at him. He would be the bad guy of all time.

The cigar smoker folded his arms and allowed the injustice of it all full reign over his soul. His thoughts boiled.

Did he not get a seat in the smoking section? He did.

Do they allow you to smoke cigars in the smoking section? They do.

Does he need a cigar? Oh sweet Jesus, he needs a cigar.

Will he be allowed to smoke a cigar? He will not.

He sank sullenly into the seat and entertained the idea of locking the little girl in the washroom.

The woman in the window seat finished her cigarette and said to the little girl, "Jennifer, come here." She helped Jennifer slide over and sit on her lap. "Jennifer," the mother instructed her, "look at the clouds."

Jennifer looked out the window of the airplane and looked *down* at the clouds. The little girl immediately began to sob and repeat in a frightened voice, "We're upside down! We're upside down!"

The cigar smoker turned toward the noise and coolly observed the little girl's panic. He thought to himself, "All her life this little kid has been standing on the ground looking up at the clouds. Now she is over the clouds looking down. She naturally thinks she is upside down." But he decided that it was not his place to say anything.

Jennifer's mother was the soul of logic. She explained to her, "We are in an airplane, Jennifer. When you are in an airplane, you go up in the air. When you go up in the air, you go over the clouds. So you see we are not upside down. We are right side up." And then from the mother's mouth came a conclusion that she was obviously not prepared to admit but which she could not avoid: "The clouds are upside down."

To which Jennifer replied, her sobs deepening, "We're upside down! We're upside down!"

The mother pressed the button for the cabin attendant and down the aisle came a trained and confident stewardess, prepared for any eventuality. She leaned over the cigar smoker and said in a voice of syrup to the little girl, "What's your name?"

"Jennifer," the girl whimpered.

"What's the matter, Jennifer?"

"We're upside down."

"No we're not, honey," the flight attendant assured her. Then she talked about her experience of flying and that sometimes she got afraid too, but that really there was nothing to worry about because the captain knew what he was doing, and what she found often helped was some Coca-Cola and some peanuts, and that she was going to get some and bring them back to her, and then she would see that there was no reason to cry.

The cabin attendant retreated down the aisle, smiling.

Jennifer sobbed, "We're upside down! We're upside down!"

Jennifer's mother, leaving reason, resorted to discipline. She picked the little girl off her lap and planted her firmly back in the middle seat. "Sit there and be good," she warned.

Jennifer sat there, holding her thin knees and making soft crying noises that anyone with ear to hear could pick up.

The cigar smoker heard. He leaned over to the little girl and said, "Jennifer, you are upside down!"

The little girl looked up at him in grateful recognition.

"But it's OK," said the cigar smoker. "It's OK."

Jennifer climbed over the arm of her seat and sat in the cigar-smoker's lap. And for a moment before her mother could rescue her, for one dazzling moment comparable to when an airplane breaks out of the darkened clouds into the sun, the cigar smoker knew he really didn't need the cigar.

Lord Love-A-Duck

The Inspired Imagination

> On the same day Jesus saw a man performing a work on the sabbath. He said to him, "Man, if you know what you are doing, you are blessed. But if you do not know what you are doing, you are cursed."
>
> Codex D of the Gospel of Luke 6:5

The Answering Imagination

From April to October, every evening at five, the ducks arrived. By seven they were gone.

"Here come the ducks," Tom, who lived on the third-floor center section of the condominium, would announce every evening.

"They are Canadian geese, dear." His wife, Marge, would correct him every evening.

"Just in time for cocktails," Tom would respond and rub his hands together.

The ducks could be seen at a distance in the sky. They looked as if they were coming in on the clouds. They flew in perfect, squadron formation and landed in "the drink" with honks and hoots, congratulating one another on their successful arrival.

"The drink" was the body of water which was the centerpiece of the condominium complex. It was too little to be called a lake and too large to be called a pond, so the people called it the drink. Three buildings of seven floors each surrounded the drink. They cupped it like a pair of hands. Willows wept along the bank.

Each apartment in the three buildings had a balcony which overlooked the drink. And most of the people gathered on their balconies around five to have a predinner cocktail and greet their evening visitors from the sky.

The ducks were everybody's guests.

Once the ducks had landed, they paddled about in different directions like tourists who had just gotten off a bus. On the land, they waddled this way and that, their rear ends doing Mae West imitations.

Their presence kept the conversation going. "You should never give a duck a bath," Janice, in six center, shouted over to Alice in six right. "The soap ruins the oil in their feathers; and when they land in the water, they sink and drown."

Phyllis, in five center, overhead this and said to her husband, "Can ducks drown?"

"Why don't you go grab one by the neck, Phyllis, and jam its head under the water and see?" Fred replied without taking his eyes from the evening news on the TV.

The people fed the ducks bread. They would throw hunks from their balconies onto the ground. The ducks would scurry, their necks stretched out low to the ground, and gobble up the gifts. Their whole bodies would shake as the bread slid down their tunnel necks.

"Do ducks have stomachs?" Phyllis asked.

"How do you think they shit?" Fred countered.

"Cows have two stomachs," Phyllis stated.

Fred gave her a stern look before returning to Dan Rather.

Then one evening the scene changed. One of the ducks was limping.

"Look! One's hurt," exclaimed Marge from two center.

This got George Wilbur, in six right, off his chair. He leaned over the railing and watched the duck hobbling along.

"He doesn't seem to be in pain," said a female voice from three left.

"Do ducks cry?" asked Phyllis.

"I have to go to the bathroom," said Fred.

"Throw the bread near the gimpy duck," commanded George Wilbur, who was a take-charge guy.

The condominium dwellers obeyed. They threw bread directly in front of the limping duck, but hurry as he might, he could not beat the other ducks to it. He went breadless, night after night.

The people were outraged. The gluttony of the other ducks disgusted them. They all agreed that this was the animal kingdom at its worst.

"Here come those selfish ducks," Tom would announce every evening around five.

"Selfish Canadian geese, dear," Marge would correct him.

"Just in time for cocktails." Tom would rub his hands.

On Thursday, after a full week of watching the gimpy duck go without bread, George Wilbur decided to skip his cocktail. Phyllis saw him first.

"Does George Wilbur know what he's doing?"

"George Wilbur never knows what he's doing," said Fred.

"Look at him."

George Wilbur was hiding among the hanging branches of one of the weeping willows. He was wearing a pair of winter gloves and he had a large net in both hands. He looked like a fowler who had escaped from an Old Testament psalm.

When the ducks landed on the water, the entire building leaned over their balcony railings and watched in silence. Once on land the ducks began their mindless, bobbing stroll. The gimp made his appearance.

George's first toss missed. The ducks honked and ran and flew. On his second toss, the net floated perfectly through the air and snared the limping duck.

"Got you, you son of a bitch." George carefully scooped him up from behind. The duck went peaceably.

"I'm taking him to the vet," he yelled up to the spectators.

One and all, they applauded.

They kept him in the utility room in six center overnight. The woman came in with bread soaked in milk. The gimpy duck guzzled greedily.

"Do ducks get fat, like, you know, overweight?" Phyllis asked.

No one answered.

In the morning George put on his winter gloves, placed

the duck in a large cardboard box with air holes poked in, loaded the box into the back of his station wagon, and went to the vet.

George sat in the waiting room, proud that he cared enough to do something.

After a half-hour the veterinarian returned. "You're right. This duck has a very bad leg. The cartilage is rotting away. Some damn fools have been feeding him too much white bread."

Shame on Al

The Inspired Imagination

> At that time, some were present who told him about the Galileans whose blood Pilate had mixed with their sacrifices. Jesus said in reply: "Do you think that these Galileans were the greatest sinners in Galilee just because they suffered this? By no means!"
>
> Luke 13:1–3

The Answering Imagination

Al had died jogging, and his friends knew why.

"You don't start to jog when you're fifty-three," one said.

"I read somewhere that you should start off walking fast and gradually build up to running," said another.

"Let's face it," chimed in a third. "Al's whole lifestyle was heart-attack material. He was a compulsive overachiever. He hadn't taken a real vacation in over three years."

"True," the other two said in unison.

Now that they had buried Al with blame, the future opened, endless, before these three pilgrims—if only they were cautious.

Paint The Other Side

The Inspired Imagination

> On one occasion Jesus spoke thus: "Father, Lord of heaven and earth, to you I offer praise; for what you have hidden from the learned and the clever you have revealed to the merest children . . . Come to me, all you who are weary and find life burdensome, and I will refresh you. Take my yoke upon your shoulders and learn from me, for I am gentle and humble of heart. Your souls will find rest, for my yoke is easy and my burden light."
>
> Matthew 11:25, 28–30

The Answering Imagination

Claire and Tom were going to be married twenty-five years on Friday. They decided against a party. They had a slew of good reasons: whom to invite, where to have it, how to be serious about not wanting gifts. Besides, it would cost a fortune.

A week earlier Claire, suspicious that her sister Ann might be cooking up something, phoned her with their decision. "Tom and I will probably just go out to dinner." Then she added the obligatory "A candlelight dinner." There was silence on the other end. "So no surprises. OK, Ann?"

More silence. Then, "Caught my thought, did you? Well, OK, If that's the way you two want it."

From the tone of her voice Claire knew she had surprised her. Ann had not given the anniversary a thought until she mentioned it. She had been the maid of honor too.

The lone voice for a party was Joyce, their eighteen-year-old daughter. The single reason which she put forward as if it would change everything was "It only happens once." This observation left Tom and Claire speechless. "Well," Claire finally said, reaching into the storehouse of stock parental responses, "your father and I have already decided."

"Jeez," said Joyce. "You'd think it was a burden."

Claire got sick Thursday night and spent Friday on the sofa in a housecoat with a box of Kleenex. She blew her nose, watched soaps, and pondered.

When Tom got home from work, he took one look at her curled up on the sofa, her nose red, her face without expression. "Psychosomatic?" he ventured.

"Why can't we get worked up for this, Tom? It only happens once."

"Is there something wrong with us?" Tom said to the air between them.

"Not that I know of." Claire pushed her hair back.

"Me neither." Tom plopped into the chair he had plopped into every evening for twenty-five years. "Well, maybe this is just how it is after twenty-five years."

"Oh God," sighed Claire at the prospect of this blah extending indefinitely into the future. It was the first real prayer she had uttered in years.

"Surprise!" Joyce jumped from the hallway. In her hands was a rectangular box wrapped with anniversary paper.

"It looks like a half-gallon of booze to me," Tom said. "Maybe we should stay home and get drunk."

"Wrong!" said Joyce.

Next came an operatic "Happy Anniversary" accompanied by a dance that combined ballet and bugaloo. On the final chord, Joyce deposited the box in Claire's lap. The Kleenex was snatched away.

Claire opened the card. On the cover was an unshaven man, in T-shirt, baggy pants, and slippers, plopped down in front of the T.V. His right hand held a can of beer which rested on his potbelly. At the other end of the sofa was a woman in curlers, face cream, and housecoat, darning a sock. Her finger stuck through a hole in the sock and she was staring stupidly at it. The inscription read: "To a still handsome man and a still beautiful woman on their silver anniversary."

Claire glared at Joyce.

"Look inside, Mom."

Inside was a picture of a teenage girl, ratty hair, braces, freckles, pimples, jeans with a hole in the knee, and a T-shirt which read "Puke!" The inscription read: "From your still beautiful daughter."

Claire let out a "short snort," which is what Tom calls "her laugh when she is trying not to." She passed the card to Tom.

"I don't remember posing for this," he said, staring at the potbellied man on the front.

"Wrong!" said Joyce. "Open it, Mom."

Claire carefully unwrapped the box and unlatched its notched cardboard top.

"What is this?" she exclaimed as she pulled out the tissue-wrapped object.

"Careful, Mom."

In Claire's hands was a large, Waterford crystal vase. The last light of the day was streaming through the west window. It caught the vase and reflected along each cut of the glass. The sun danced on the crystal.

"Oh God, it's beautiful," said Claire softly.

Tom was stunned. He could think of nothing to say, so he said, "Where did you get the money?"

"I robbed a bank."

"What? No flowers?" was his comeback.

Joyce disappeared. Tom reached for the Kleenex.

Joyce was back as quick as she left. In her hands were yellow mums. She put them on the table, ran into the kitchen, filled the gravy pitcher with water, and poured the water in the vase. She arranged the flowers one by one and fluffed them carefully.

"Renoir or Matisse or somebody says you must carefully arrange flowers," Joyce instructed. She put the vase on the table between the sofa where her mother was and the chair her father sat in.

"Then when you are done," she continued, "you turn the flowers around and paint the other side." She turned the vase around so that Tom and Claire both saw the side that was hidden from them. "There," Joyce said.

"Who told you that?" Tom asked.

"My art teacher."

"Smart man that Renoir or Matisse or somebody."

"Come here," said her mother. Claire kissed her. "Thanks, darling. It means more than you know."

"My turn," said Tom. Joyce came over and sat in her father's lap. He kissed her nose like he used to do when she was a little girl. "The last eighteen were the best of the twenty-five," he said.

"I agree," said Claire.

For a long time they all looked at the vase. There did not seem to be a need to say anything.

Finally, Claire bounced up from the sofa. "Make reservations for three at someplace expensive. I'm going to get dressed."

She walked down the hall to her bedroom, and from the view her husband and daughter had, it looked like her housecoat lifted off the floor with each step.

"Is Mom skipping?" asked Joyce incredulously.

"Your mother always skips," said the man who had been married twenty-five years.

Let Them Be Who They Will Be

The Inspired Imagination

"A man had two sons.

The younger of them said to his father, 'Father, give me the share of the estate that is coming to me.'

So the father divided up the property.

Some days later this younger son collected all his belongings and went off to a distant land, where he squandered his money on dissolute living.

After he had spent everything, a great famine broke out in that country and he was in dire need. So he attached himself to one of the propertied class of the place, who sent him to his farm to take care of the pigs. He longed to fill his belly with the husks that were fodder for the pigs, but no one made a move to give him anything.

Coming to his senses at last, he said: 'How many hired hands at my father's place have more than enough to eat, while here I am starving! I will break away and return to my father, and say to him, Father, I have sinned against God and against you; I no longer deserve to be called your son. Treat me like one of your hired hands.' With that he set off for his father's house.

While he was still a long way off, his father caught sight of him and was deeply moved. He ran out to meet him, threw his arms around his neck, and kissed him.

The son said to him, 'Father, I have sinned against God and against you; I no longer deserve to be called your son.'

The father said to his servants, 'Quick! Bring out the finest robe and put it on him; put a ring on his finger and shoes on his feet. Take the fatted calf and kill it. Let us eat and celebrate because this son of mine was dead and has come back to life. He was lost and is found.'

Then the celebration began.

Meanwhile the elder son was out on the land. As he neared the house on his way home, he heard the sound of music and dancing. He called one of the servants and asked him the reason for the dancing and music.

The servant answered, 'Your brother is home, and your father has killed the fatted calf because he has him back in good health.'

The son grew angry at this and would not go in; but his father came out and began to plead with him.

He said to his father in reply: 'For years now I have slaved for you. I never disobeyed one of your orders, yet you never gave me so much as a kid goat to celebrate with my friends. Then, when this son of yours returns after having gone through your property with loose women, you kill the fatted calf for him.'

'My son,' replied the father, 'you are with me always, and everything I have is yours. But we had to celebrate and rejoice! This brother of yours was dead, and has come back to life. He was lost, and is found.' "

Luke 15:11–32

The Answering Imagination

The Younger Son

On beef,
the meat around the bone is best
On woman,
though, I prefer the plump parts,

What a feast my father throws!
O belly, we're back!
No more watch and rumble
while the swine swill and snort
and I bite through my lip and drool
for a munch on one of their carob pods.
But a love slap on their unclean rumps!
They made me remember my own trough—
DADDY.

I rehearsed a speech,
a mumble masterpiece.
With a mouth turned down,
an eyeful of mist,
repentant as a whore with clap:
I whimper:
"Father, I have sinned against heaven
and against thee." (voice falters)
(Daddy, your little boy has done wrong
and he's so sorry that he'll never do it again.
Really, he won't.)

John Shea

"Do not take me back as a son:
take me back as a hired hand."
(But TAKE ME BACK,
my belly and I do beg,
you large-lardered,
stuffed-saddlebagged,
wine-drenched
old Daddy.)

Grovel a little to guzzle a lot:
crawl on your belly to feed it.
That is my philosophy.

But the old man upstaged me.
He fell upon me in mid-sentence
ruining my clever act.
But the script was magic.
A robe, ring, and sandals
suddenly appeared;
and this feast fell from heaven.
It was like I was,
what can I say,
a long lost son,
a dead man come back to life.

But I suspect Father is up to something.
No one can be that happy
to see the return of an appetite
that swallowed half an inheritance.
But, then again, I always was his favorite
and I could make him dance to any tune I piped.
Gushy old men are my specialty.
Anyway, the calf is succulent.
I have what I want,
and that is what I have always wanted.

The Older Brother

All these years!
Even the servant boy sensed it.
He would not look at me
as he told me the news:
"Your brother is home,
and your father has killed the fatted calf
because he has him back safe and sound."
He has had ME home—
all these years—
and no music ever greeted ME
as I dragged in
from our fields.
All those mornings!
With him coughing up his night phlegm
and complaining of the cold,
and me throwing a blanket around his bones,
and sitting him on a bench in the sun.
All those days! With him staring off in the opposite direction
of wherever I was,
growing weary from watching
for the one who does not come,
and me looking up from the earth
to find his back blocking the sky.
All those harvests!
With me, giddy as a child who had found a coin,
yelling for him to come
see the hundredfold crop and sagging vines,
and him coming and sighing
like the wheat was dust and grapes were rocks.
All those nights!
With him droning a prayer

and nodding over his food,
and forgetting to bless me before bed.
And me waiting for the embrace
he was saving,
hoping for the words
he was hoarding,
eager for an unfeigned arm
around my shoulder,
for a kiss strong enough
to bring blood to my cheek.

Now he tells me that
all these years
we have been
together
and have become one.
"You have been with me always;
and all I have is yours."
I need more, Father,
I need you to run to ME
out of breath and heart-bursting,
not as you are now with your sensible "Now see here" logic
about the fittingness of feasting
for someone else.

All these years!

The Father

I have two sons,
neither of whom wants ME for a father.
So they make me into the father they want.

One makes me into a pimp for his belly.
He thinks he tricks me into concessions,
cons a calf from a sentimental old fool.

The Spirit Master

He credits my dancing to his piping:
but the music I hear has another source.
He is always empty
so my fullness is hidden from him.
His cunning gives him no rest
so my peace eludes him.

He secretly seizes in the night
what I freely offer in the day.
He wants a father he can steal from.
Instead he has me,
 a vine with more wine
than he can drink.
It is hard for him to forgive me
for providing more than he can plunder.
I am abundance.
He must learn to live with it.

The other one counts my kisses.
He wants me to count his.
"For two days ploughing,
take this hug.
For a plentiful harvest,
receive this blessing."
He is so unsure of himself,
he cannot share my assurance.
He lives by measuring what he does not have.
An eye anywhere else
is an eye lost to him.
He thinks I take him for granted;
but I lean on him like a staff.
He is the privileged companion
of my morning pain and evening praise.
I would allow no one else to see

the stumble of my memory,
the embarrassment of my body.
But he credits my love to his loyalty.
He wants a father, indentured to him,
paying him back in affection
for his backbreaking labor.
Instead he has me,
an ancient tree with its own soil.
He does not understand
that he cannot calm his panic with a bargain.
There will be no chain between us.
I freely tie my wrist to his.

I have two sons.
Wherever they are,
I go to meet them.
I am their father.
But I am who I am.
Let them be
who they will be.

EPILOGUE

A Down-and-Out Disciple Meets His Match

It was a wind-blasted winter evening, close to midnight, in the Year of Our Lord Nineteen Hundred and Ninety-Six and the doors of the apartment were locked. Inside, the disciple was eating popcorn and riffling through the Gospels. He was reading at top speed, flipping pages, hoping a word, a sentence, a story would make him stop. He was looking for something, but he wasn't sure what it was.

Suddenly Jesus appeared and sat down in the chair opposite him. The disciple blanched. He shook, rubbed his eyes, looked away, and looked back. Jesus stubbornly stayed put. Finally Jesus said, "Got anything to eat?"

"I get it," said the disciple. "That's what you did after you rose. When the disciples thought you were a ghost, you asked for something to eat. It reassured them you were real."

"I was hungry. What is this stuff?"

"Popcorn." The disciple passed the bowl over to Jesus. "Try some, Lord," he said, and the words sounded absolutely ludicrous. He consoled himself with the thought that he didn't say, "Mister Lord."

Jesus took one piece of popcorn and looked at it as though he were examining a diamond with an eyepiece.

"Wonderful shape," Jesus said, "and each one is just a little different. I like them."

The disciple became a little uneasy. He had never heard popcorn referred to as "them." And how did he know he liked them if he hadn't tasted them?

Jesus put one piece in his mouth and chewed it carefully for close to a minute. The disciple grabbed a handful.

"Not enough salt," Jesus finally said.

"Salt is not good for you," warned the disciple.

"I was always one for a lot of salt," said Jesus. "Hey!" Jesus raised his finger in the air like he was about to give a teaching. "Has anyone tried putting butter on this stuff?"

"It's been done. But butter's not good for you either."

"You are a very careful person," said Jesus.

"Thanks," said the disciple. "Here, have some more." The disciple raised the bowl of popcorn off the table and offered it to Jesus.

"No thanks."

"You are the only person I know who can eat only one piece of popcorn and stop."

"Of course. I'm God," Jesus said, and laughed.

The disciple did his best to chuckle.

"How come when YOU eat popcorn," Jesus said as he stroked his chin, "you try to get as much into your mouth as possible, and it spills out, and you have to pick it off our shirt, and put it back in your mouth?"

"Oh God, I knew this was going to happen."

"Why does everybody say that when I'm around?" Asked Jesus, a bit irritated. "What did you know was going to happen?"

"You notice everything and make remarks."

"You don't like to be noticed?"

"As a matter of fact, I don't."

The disciple closed his eyes. When he opened them, Jesus was still there, and smiling.

"Why did you come?"

"To teach you how to eat popcorn." Jesus looked pleased with himself.

The disciple looked down at the bowl of popcorn on the table. "Are you going to toy with me?" he said, angrily.

"I am not toying with you. I always come to seek what is lost, and when people are searching through my story at midnight like it was a medicine cabinet, it is usually a sign they are lost."

"Like hell I'm lost!" the disciple shouted.

"Like hell you're not!" Jesus shouted back.

Their eyes locked. The disciple was the first to look away.

"It's a mild case of midlife crisis. I'll be over it in a couple of months." The disciple gave a "what can I tell you" shrug of his shoulders.

"Is that what they are calling temptation these days—midlife crisis?"

The disciple laughed in spite of himself.

Slowly Jesus reached over to the bowl of popcorn, took one piece, and popped it into his mouth. Jesus' obvious enjoyment made the disciple shake his head.

"Even God can't eat only one piece of popcorn," said the disciple.

"Especially God," said Jesus. "Try some."

The disciple instinctively took a handful of popcorn, but then let some fall back into the bowl. He put the pieces in his mouth two or three at a time.

When both of them had finished chewing, Jesus said in a very gentle voice, "You have been with me now a long time, and you are wondering whether it is all worth it. You've got your hand on the plow and your head on backwards."

"It used to be easy," the disciple said, rummaging his memory. "You died for me, and I owed you, so I signed up. But, now I ask, who asked you to die for me?"

"My Father, of course."

"I never asked you to."

"You wouldn't. You're the type who doesn't like to be noticed. You would rather die yourself."

The disciple's head snapped straight back like someone had just pounded a fist into his chin. Before he could respond, Jesus had a suggestion.

"I think you follow me because you like my teachings."

"You've got to be kidding. Some of them make sense. But most of them I don't get, and all of them are too hard."

"Name one."

"Anyone who lusts after a woman in his heart has already committed adultery."

"Name another."

The disciple laughed. Jesus laughed at the disciple's laughter.

"You know, one of the worst times," Jesus' voice was mellow and reflective, "was after my Father raised me. Mary went to the tomb and found two angels but not my body. The angels asked, 'Woman, why are you weeping?' She tells them she doesn't know what has happened to my body and it is driving her crazy with grief. ALL THE TIME I'M STANDING RIGHT BEHIND HER. She turns and looks right at me. I decide to ape the angels. 'Woman,' I say, 'why are you weeping?' Then I point to myself like a little boy on stage and say in gentle and joyous mockery, 'Who is it that you are looking for?' It was a little showy, but I was happy to see her.

"But she says, 'Sir.' She calls me 'Sir.' That 'Sir' killed me a second time. I realized that she didn't recognize me. She thinks I'm the gardener and wants to know if I have any information about the whereabouts of my own body. I cry out in her pain and mine, 'Mary!' And she knows me. It was only when I said her name that she found my body. That's what I meant about lust. You know what I mean?"

"No."

"Think about it."

"Tell me about your Father."

"Love to. I was floating on my back in the Sea of Galilee. The water was holding me up effortlessly. It was buoying me up and stretching me out and, as I later reflected, getting me ready to receive. I was looking straight up into the sky. No clouds. Just a blue so deep it was hard to look at. When suddenly the sky fell into me. I felt like infinite azure. It was my Father playing around. Have you ever felt like infinite azure?"

"Sometimes."

"Have I ever made you feel like infinite azure?"

"Not in a long time."

"How about finite aquamarine?"

"Don't mock me!"

"A definitely limited indigo?"

"Cut it out!"

"Look!" Jesus grabbed his disciple's shoulders and looked into his eyes. "You are drowning in self-pity. Play with me. I can't take dismal disciples."

The disciple put his head down. He did not look at Jesus.

After a couple of minutes, Jesus asked, "What are you thinking about?"

"You tell me. I thought you could read hearts."

"Only when the wind is right. What's going on?"

"Why don't you just go away?"

"I can't. I told you. I came to seek what is lost. I'm the Messiah."

"The scholars say you didn't use titles for yourself."

"You read too much, and you are trying to get me off the subject like that woman I met by the well."

"What's the subject?"

"You."

"Well, did you use titles?"

"Is there any mule in your lineage? OK, I'll tell you. Back in those days, people were overeager to believe in messiahs, so I didn't mention it. Today, people are overeager not to believe in messiahs, so I say it. I offended them by not saying it, and I see I embarrass you by saying it."

"You do not. I am a believer."

"You are an embarrassed believer."

"Well, wouldn't you be?" The disciple stood up and walked away from the table. "Here I am, a modern person, looking to a first-century Jew for the meaning of life? There are a lot of other models around."

"Someone a little more in step with the times?" asked Jesus.

"Right!"

"Like Lee Iacocca."

"You're mocking me again."

"You are thinking of divorcing me quietly, aren't you?"

"It has crossed my mind."

"My friend, you need more chutzpah. Blessed are those who are not embarrassed by me."

The disciple sat back down at the table. There were no words for a long time.

Then Jesus said, "There was a bank robber who planned a heist for a long time. He had worked out the details and was ready to go. But when he got to the bank teller's window, he suddenly panicked and asked directions to the washroom."

"Hah! You're saying I can't carry through what I set out to do."

"I'm saying risk the salt on the popcorn."

"Jesus," the disciple said in an exasperated voice, "I'm going to lay it on the line. You walk too fast; I can't keep up."

"Better to be out of breath behind me than ahead of everyone else."

"I want a more moderate Master so I can be a better disciple."

"You are a perfect disciple—you cannot receive my death, you cannot live up to my teachings, my father scares you, and you do not know how to eat popcorn."

"That may be accurate but it is hardly perfect."

"My friend, that is the way of the earth beyond the earth. Why live out of something as small as you are? Love me because I am large enough to betray. But I do not think you are happy in the land of mercy."

"God, you are a bittersweet experience."

"There is no lie in me."

"Why do you say things so harshly?"

"Peter used to say that I was the only one who could say 'God loves you' and get everybody mad."

The disciple laughed. So did Jesus.

"You laugh at the right places," said Jesus. Then suddenly he asked, "So, are you going to stick around?"

"Where will I go? You have the words of eternal life."

"No fair stealing Peter's lines."

"Will YOU stick around with someone like me?" The disciple sighed like some great buildup of pressure had been released.

"Is that what this is all about?" asked Jesus. "You know all things, you know that I love you."

"No fair stealing Peter's lines. Why did you say that?"

"When Peter said it to me, it blew me away. I hoped it might do the same for you."

"But I don't know everything."

"You know enough."

"I know that even when I want you to go away, I don't want you to go away."

"East of Eden we call that love," said the Master, and tears ran freely down his face.

In imitation of his Master, the disciple cried.

For a long time there were no words, only the silence of communication.

"You know," Jesus finally said, "after Lazarus came back to life, he told me that what woke him up in the tomb was the sound of my tears."

"I can believe it," said the disciple.

Jesus smiled and reached for a third piece of popcorn. The disciple also took a piece. Jesus closed his eyes to savor better. The faithful disciple did likewise. When the disciple opened his eyes, Jesus was gone. But there was such an inner, incredible lightness to his being, that the disciple knew where he had vanished to.

ENDNOTES

Preface

1. Karl Rahner, *The Love of Jesus and the Love of Neighbor* (New York: Crossroad, 1983), p. 23.
2. Leonardo Boff, *Salvation and Liberation* (Maryknoll, New York: 1984), p. 2.
3. Herwig Arts, *With Your Whole Soul* (New York: Paulist Press, 1978), p. 15.
4. Cf. John Shea, *An Experience Named Spirit* (Allen TX: Thomas More Publishing, 1983), Chapter Two.
5. Rahner, *op. cit.*, p. 18.
6. *Ibid.*, p. 24.

Chapter One

1. Paul VI, *Apostolic Exhortation Evangelii Nuntiandi* (New York: Daughters of St. Paul, 1975), p. 13.
2. *The Evangelization of the Modern World,* U.S.C.C. 1973, pp. 1–2.
3. Summary taken from Rev. Robert J. Hater, *The Relationship Between Evangelization and Catechesis,* NCCD, 1981, p. 8.
4. A fine article that explores *Evangelii Nuntiandi* in a Latin American context is Jon Sobrino, *The True Church and the Poor* (Maryknoll, New York: Orbis Books, 1984), pp. 253–301.
5. Martin Lang, *Acquiring Our Image of God* (New York: Paulist Press, 1983).
6. Quoted in the introduction to Flannery O'Connor's *Everything That Rises Must Converge* (New York: Farrar, Straus, and Giroux, 1965), p. xi.
7. Anthony de Mello, *The Song of the Bird* (Chicago: Loyola University Press, 1982), pp. 182–83.
8. Alice Walker, *The Color Purple* (New York: Pocket Books, 1982), pp. 202–204.
9. Peter Roche de Coppens, *The Nature and Use of Ritual* (University Press of America, 1979), p. 31.

Chapter Two

1. Edward Schillebeeckx in conversation with Huub Oosterhuis and Piet Hoogeveen, *God Is New Each Moment* (New York: The Seabury Press, 1983), p. 1.
2. H. A. Williams, *True Resurrection* (Springfield, Illinois: Templegate Publishers, 1972), pp. 10–11.
3. Cf. John Shea, *An Experience Named Spirit,* (Allen TX: Thomas More Publishing, 1983), Chapter One.
4. Quoted in Avery Dulles, "How Can Christian Faith Be Justified Today?" in *Communio,* Vol. 2 (1975), p. 346.
5. Raymond Brown, *A Crucified Christ In Holy Week* (Collegeville, Minnesota: The Liturgical Press, 1986), p. 71.
6. Cf. John Shea, "Does Baby Jesus Believe in Santa Claus?" in *U.S. Catholic* (December 1980).
7. Schillebeeckx, *op. cit.,* p. 2.
8. G. K. Chesterton, *The Everlasting Man* (New York: Dodd, Mead, & Company, 1925), p. 202.
9. *Ibid.,* pp. 222–23.
10. Caryll Houselander, *The Risen Christ* (New York: Sheed and Ward, 1958), Chapter Three.

Chapter Three

1. Quoted in Leonardo Boff, *Jesus Christ Liberator* (Maryknoll, New York: Orbis Books, 1978), p. 99.
2. Quoted in Frans Jozef van Beeck, *Christ Proclaimed* (New York: Paulist Press, 1979), p. 228.
3. Dulles, pp. 349–350.
4. Edward Schillebeeckx in conversation with Huub Oosterhuis and Piet Hoogeveen, *God Is New Each Moment* (New York: The Seabury Press, 1983), p. 20.
5. George Bernard Shaw, "Preface on the Prospects of Christianity" (New York: Brentano's, 1916), p. xcvii.
6. Cf. William Thompson, *The Jesus Debate* (New York: Paulist Press, 1985), Chapter Five.

7. Elizabeth Johnson, "The Theological Relevance of the Historical Jesus: A Debate and a Thesis," in *The Thomist*, Vol. 48 (January, 1984), p. 9.
8. Cf. James Mackey, *Jesus: The Man and the Myth* (New York: Paulist Press, 1979), p. 195.
9. Joseph Fitzmyer, *A Christological Catechism* (New York: Paulist Press, 1981), p. 85.
10. G. K. Chesterton, *The Everlasting Man* (New York: Dodd, Mead, & Company, 1925), p. 248.
11. *Ibid.,* p. 247.
12. *Ibid.,* p. 249.
13. *Ibid.,* p. 248.
14. Edward Schillebeeckx, "The 'God of Jesus' and the 'Jesus of God'" in *Concilium: 93—Jesus Christ and Human Freedom* (New York: Herder and Herder, 1974), p. 124.
14. van Beeck, *op. cit.,* p. 483.
15. John Haught, *The Cosmic Adventure* (New York: Paulist Press, 1984), p. 160.
16. James Breech, *The Silence of Jesus* (Philadelphia: Fortress Press, 1983), pp. 86–99.
17. Quoted in Conrad Hyers, *The Comic Vision and the Christian Faith* (New York: The Pilgrim Press, 1981), p 114.
18. Quoted in van Beeck, *op. cit.,* p. 290.
19. Cf. Thompson, *op. cit.,* p. 197.
20. Cf. John Shea, *An Experience Named Spirit* (Allen TX: Thomas More Publishing, 1983), pp. 184–194.
21. Hannah Arendt, *The Human Condition* (Chicago, 1958), p. 241. Quoted in Raymond Studzinski, "Remember and Forgive: Psychological Dimensions of Forgiveness," in *Concilium*, Vol. 184 (1986), p. 12.
22. Jon Sobrino, "Latin America: Place of Sin and Place of Forgiveness," in *Concilium,* Vol. 184 (1986), p. 53.
23. Cf. Rudolf Pesch, "Jesus, a Free Man" in *Concilium,* Vol. 93 (1974), pp. 56–70.
24. Sebastian Moore, *The Fire and the Rose Are One* (New York: The Seabury Press, 1980), p. 78.

25. Breech, *op. cit.,* p. 97.
26. Cf. *ibid.*, pp. 22–31.
27. Cf. Frithjof Bergmann, *On Being Free* (Notre Dame, Indiana: University of Notre Dame Press, 1977), pp. 15–40.
28. van Beeck, *op. cit.,* p. 418.
29. Quoted in George Stroup, *Jesus Christ for Today* (Philadelphia: The Westminster Press, 1982), p. 22.
30. T. S. Eliot, *The Wasteland and Other Poems* (New York: Harcourt Brace Jovanovich, 1934), pp. 69–70.
31. Flannery O'Connor, *Wise Blood* (New York: Signet Books, 1964), p. 16.
32. Annie Dillard, "God in the Doorway," from *Teaching A Stone To Talk* (New York: Harper & Row, 1982), p. 140.
33. *Ibid.,* p. 141.
34. Rahner, p. 17.

Chapter Four

1. Jaroslav Pelikan, *Jesus Through the Centuries* (New Haven and London: Yale University Press, 1985).
2. Quoted in Pelikan, *ibid.,* p. 2.
3. van Beeck, pp. 144–228. I am just borrowing this basic framework from van Beeck. His "working of it" is more sophisticated and nuanced than I am presenting.
4. Cf. Joseph A. Fitzmeyer, "The Biblical Commission and Christology," in *Theological Studies* 46 (1985), pp. 407–78.
5. Williams, pp. 177–78.
6. Quoted in Williams, *ibid.,* p. 179
7. Aaron Milavec, *To Empower As Jesus Did: Acquiring Spiritual Power Through Apprenticeship* (New York: The Edwin Mellen Press, 1982), pp. 105–106.
8. J. K. Kadowaki, *Zen and the Bible* (London: Routledge & Kegan Paul, 1980), pp. 71–72.
9. John Cobb, "A Whiteheadian Christology," in *Process Philosophy and Christian Thought,* pp. 395–96.

10. Anthony de Mello, *One Minute Wisdom* (New York: Doubleday & Co., 1986), p. 120.
11. Michael Polanyi, *Personal Knowledge* (New York: Harper & Row, 1964), p. 53.
12. David K. O'Rourke, *A Process Called Conversion* (New York: Doubleday & Co., 1985), p. 63.

Chapter Five

1. Milavec, p. 247.
2. Quoted in Royce Gordon Gruenler, *New Approaches To Jesus And The Gospels* (Grand Rapids, Michigan: Baker Books House,
3. *Ibid.,* p. 148.
4. *Ibid.,* p. 149.
5. Ben Meyer, *The Aims Of Jesus* (London: SCM Press, 1979), pp. 250–51.
6. Kadowaki, p. 93.
7. Cf. Robert Tannehill, *The Sword Of His Mouth* (Philadelphia: Fortress Press, 1975).
8. Kadowaki, *op. cit.,* p. 96.
9. Mary Ann Tolbert, *Perspective On The Parables* (Philadelphia: Fortress Press, 1979), p. 70.
10. Earl Breech, "Kingdom of God and the Parables of Jesus," in *Semeia* 10–12 (1978), p. 34.

Chapter Six

1. Conrad Hyers, *The Comic Vision And The Christian Faith* (New York: The Pilgrim Press, 1981), p. 36.
2. *Ibid.,* p. 37.
3. de Mello, *Song,* pp. 70–71.
4. Quoted by Breech, *Silence*, p. 47.
5. Kadowaki, pp. 54–62.